te of Creswells walke
The Orcharde
The garden Plott
Castle
The Lowe grounde
Part of Eaton

Royal Castle, Rebel Town 1981
has been published as a Limited
Edition of which this is

Number   77

A complete list of the
original subscribers is
printed at the back of the book

Royal Castle, Rebel Town

A	*The :Divell*	G	*Cor : Holland*
B	*Olever:Cromwell*	H	*I: Iones*
C	*Io : Bradshaw Pres:*	I	*Lisle*
D	*Tho: Scott*	K	*Say*
E	*Coll: Harrison*	L	*Hugh Petters*
F	*Coll:Barksted*	M	*I :Goodwin*

FRONT COVER: Royalist caricature of Cromwell's Cabinet Council. Cornelius Holland, Windsor's republican MP, is on the left. (SNPG)

The Earl of Essex, Parliamentary Commander, at Windsor.
The Castle is shown on the left; the Little Park with pikemen
parading is on the right. Engraving by Wenceslaus Hollar.
Reproduced by permission of the Master and Fellows of
Magdalene College, Cambridge.

Royal Castle, Rebel Town

Puritan Windsor In Civil War & Commonwealth

by

Raymond South

Raymond South.
17 March 1981

BARRACUDA BOOKS LIMITED
BUCKINGHAM , ENGLAND
MCMLXXXI

PUBLISHED BY BARRACUDA BOOKS LIMITED
BUCKINGHAM, ENGLAND
AND PRINTED BY
BURGESS & SON (ABINGDON) LIMITED
ABINGDON, ENGLAND

BOUND BY
HAZELL, WATSON & VINEY LIMITED
AYLESBURY, ENGLAND

JACKET PRINTED BY
CHENEY & SONS LIMITED
BANBURY, OXON

LITHOGRAPHY BY
BICESTER PHOTO LITHO LIMITED
BICESTER, ENGLAND

TYPESET IN 11/11pt TIMES ROMAN
BY PERFORMANCE TYPESETTING LIMITED
MILTON KEYNES, ENGLAND

Contents

Acknowledgements

My research has taken me to many Record Offices and Libraries, including the City of London Guildhall Library, the British Library, Dr Williams' Library, the Windsor Guildhall, the Windsor Reference Library, the Berkshire Record Office, the Oxford City Library, the Oxford Union Library. I offer my sincere thanks for the help given in all these places.

Among the many friends who have helped me by reading the script and in other ways are Maurice Bond, Graham Brown, Rev David Griffiths, Judith Hunter, Ruth Newman, Gerald Parker, Rev Denis Shaw, Margaret Whitelaw.

I also owe a great debt to the following for their help in making the book known: the branch libraries at Windsor, Maidenhead and Eton, the Windsor and Eton Society, the Historical Association, the Berkshire Local History Association, the Windsor and Eton Chamber of Trade, the Middle Thames Archaeological and Historical Society, the Mid-Thames Centre of the National Trust.

Finally, my warmest thanks must go to Clive Birch of Barracuda and his staff for their unfailing encouragement and patience in seeing my book through to publication.

Caption Credits

NPG   National Portrait Gallery, London
SNPG   Scottish National Portrait Gallery, Edinburgh
Ashmole E. Ashmole *Institutions, Laws and Ceremonies of the Most Noble Order of the Garter* (1672)
TD   R.R. Tighe and J.E. Davis *Annals of Windsor* (1858)

Title calligraphy and borders by Alan Walker; design based on original Civil War pamphlets.

Introduction

History has a habit of surprising us. Through the centuries Windsor has had a close association with the monarchy—with the sole exception of the 17th century Civil War and Commonwealth period.

Every year from his accession in 1625 to 1641 Charles I held court at Windsor. Then in 1642 came the outbreak of the Civil War and in October Parliament occupied the Castle and maintained its possession throughout the 18 years to the Restoration in 1660.

Beneath the walls of the Castle was a puritan town, loyal to the parliamentary cause. In 1640 the townspeople chose two puritan MPs to represent them. One of these was the republican Cornelius Holland who reached the peak of his fame when he became a member of the Council of State in the early years of the Commonwealth.

It has been a rewarding task to portray the personalities of the Parliamentary leaders who were active in Windsor. To reconstruct the lives of the townspeople has been less easy, but we know something about many of them and there is material for further research.

Royal Castle, Rebel Town is the story of a unique episode in the history of Windsor which will, I hope, prove of interest both to the general reader and to the specialist historian. For the former I have attempted to supply sufficient background to make the local story significant. Maybe it will stimulate the desire to read more widely in what must surely be one of the most dramatic periods in English history. For the specialists I trust I have been able to incorporate enough of the original findings of my research to give the book value. What happened in Windsor is not only important in itself but throws light on what happened in many other towns.

Throughout the book quotations have normally been modernised for both spelling and punctuation. I have standardised the spelling of proper names.

I have adopted the usual practice over dates, with the year regarded as beginning on 1 January, eg: the King's execution is dated 30 Jan 1649, not 1648.

For Marjorie

9

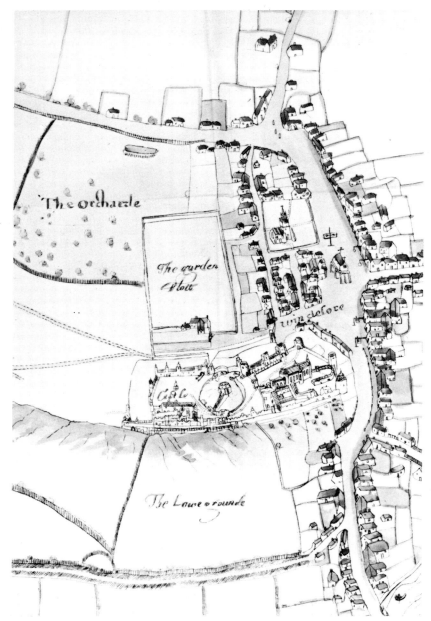

The orcharde

The garden Plott

inn before

Castle

The Lowe grounde

John Norden's View *of the Castle and Town, 1607. Beyond
the Market House are the Pillory and the old Parish Church.
The two inn signs opposite the Castle are those of the White
Hart and the Garter. (TD)*

10

Before The Storm

What an attractive little town Windsor looks in John Norden's *View* of 1607—the Castle on its hill, the houses with their bright red roofs clustered beneath the Castle walls, the Market House on its rickety legs, the swift-flowing river with its bridge and its boats. How difficult it is to imagine this as the setting for the drama enacted here in the 1640s and 50s, when the Parliamentarians were the lords of Windsor and King Charles and his Cavaliers were exiles from the royal Castle.

Seventeenth century Windsor was a small market town, smaller than most villages of the present day. The inhabitants numbered somewhere between one and two thousand at the time of the Civil War. They may even have been fewer at the beginning of the century, for a petition to the King in 1634 says that since James I came to the throne 'the Town . . . hath been well near the one half enlarged'.[1] We cannot be much more precise.

Windsor, however, was never *just* a market town, of importance only to the immediate neighbourhood. Its association with the Royal Castle made it something more. Travellers and men with business at the Court frequented Windsor. Such visitors could no longer expect to have hospitality provided for them by the generosity of the local gentry—and certainly not in the Castle itself. They must seek for it in the hostelries of the town and pay for their board and lodging out of their own pockets. Inns in fact were increasingly important. We know the names of many of them. There were the Garter and the White Hart opposite the road leading up to the Castle, the Red Lion and the Crown at the bottom of the hill, as well as the Bull, the Ram, the Black Eagle, the Cardinal's Hat, the Chequers, the Swan, the Maidenhead, the Goat, the White Lion, the Mermaid, the Bell, the Rose, the Cross Keys and the King Harry.

When the number of Windsor's inhabitants increased and more houses were needed, the town grew not outwards but inwards. In the first half of the century a row of houses, extending from the main gateway of the Castle, was built in the broad ditch right under the Castle walls. When William Herrendon, apothecary, was granted the lease of one of these houses, he had 'to keep the door through the lower room of the premises for a passage into the Castle ditch there for workmen and other persons to pass through for the amending of the Castle Wall'.[2] Below the castle escarpment and flanking the road leading to the bridge was the hamlet of Windsor Underore. It can be seen in the contemporary etchings of the Czech Wenceslaus Hollar and the paintings of the Dutch artists who frequented Windsor in the 17th century. The houses in the castle ditch and most of Windsor Underore have long since vanished, but the main lay-out of the town centre has hardly changed at all—Castle Hill, High Street, Thames Street, Peascod Street, Park Street, Sheet Street. In one or two cases the names have changed, but the pattern of the streets remains.

The houses were set amidst gardens and orchards and the country came right into the town. This is partly why Windsor has such a pleasant appearance in Norden's *View*. The by-laws of 1610 *(Orders and By Laws concerning the fields)* in fact seem more appropriate to a rural than to an urban community. The first by-law orders that 'every Landholder within the Borough shall for ever hereafter yearly and every year make and repair or cause to be made and repaired sufficiently his hedges and ditches and other fences so far as his Land or Meadow extendeth, so as to be continued in good repair until the Corn and hay of the said Meadows and fields be all Inned'. Subsequent sections regulate the pasturage of cattle, sheep and horses in the meadows and fields.[3]

The Corporation had the difficult task of maintaining in this rural environment the standards appropriate to an urban community. By the by-laws of 1635-6 pigs were not allowed to run loose in the streets. Dunghills were ordered to be removed from the streets and lanes, as well as all other obstructions to the thoroughfares, such as carts, timber, blocks, heaps of stone, or 'other offensive lumber'.

In 1629 the High Street was paved 'from the north end of the Corn Market house, and from the upper end of Peascod Street unto the upper part of a Tenement of the Mayor, Bailiffs and Burgesses adjoining unto the wall of the Castle Bridge'. The by-laws of 1635-6 provided that every shopkeeper should maintain in repair the part adjacent to his dwelling and—a noteworthy advance—'every Mayor of the Borough for the time being shall or may nominate and appoint a sufficient Scavenger for carrying away of such dust or other Rubbish as shall weekly be made and cast upon the said pavement'.[4]

No doubt many of these by-laws were well-intentioned. Whether they were observed or enforced is another matter. Certainly they did not prevent the recurrence of pestilence. The first year of the Stuarts was marked by a particularly bad outbreak of plague. The normal number of burials recorded in the parish registers varies from three to five in each month. In 1603, in the five months from July to November, there were 133, a monthly average of 26.6. In the following year a pest-house was built in Sheet Street. 1624 and 1625 were also bad years, but the scourge was never far removed from the daily lives of the townspeople. Plague in Windsor usually coincided with plague in London, underlining the close association between Windsor and the Metropolis.

Windsor, like most towns of the period, was faced with pauperism and its associated problems. Many attempts had been made to legislate in the

16th century, culminating in Elizabeth's great Poor Law of 1601. The abuse of charity was a common complaint and in Windsor, as elsewhere, the council turned to the provision of work as an additional form of poor relief. Work, as a Windsor benefactor put it, would restrain the 'lazy and vicious' from 'their ill-habits' and, better still, would involve a more economic use of man power and help the growth of trade. In 1591 it was ordered 'that all the brethren of the Hall [the members of the Corporation] and all other Inhabitants shall be assessed according to their ability by the subsidy after the rate of 12d in the pound towards levying of a stock to set the poor on work'.[5]

The proximity of the Park and Forest must have been a continual temptation to the townspeople. Alderman Matthew Day records how at the end of April 1624 he was a member of a small deputation of leading citizens who approached King James, when the latter was hunting in the Park, to pray His Majesty for financial assistance to the Vicar in the shape of 'a Canon's place in his free Chapel of Windsor', ie: St George's. What they received was an angry outburst. 'Am I any ill neighbour unto you? Do I do you any hurt? Doth my coming be any hindrance unto you? Why then do you vex me by permitting and suffering your poor to cut down and carry away my woods out of my Parks and grounds and to sell the same?'[6] It is hardly likely that the poaching activities of the townspeople were confined to inanimate objects such as timber.

Presiding over the small community that made up the borough of Windsor, *New* Windsor as it was still officially known, was the Mayor and Corporation. It is tempting to make a comparison with 20th century parish councils rather than with municipalities with their wide range of powers and responsibilities. But the Corporation of a borough, even of a small borough such as Windsor, had a status to which no modern parish council could lay claim. It had long historical traditions, extending back, in the case of Windsor, at least to Edward I's charter of 1277. Church-going, feasting and all the ephemera of civic life were integrated with these traditions. The Corporation—Mayor, Aldermen, Benchers, Brethren—numbered 28 to 30 of the 'substantialist and wisest men of the Town'.[7] And even if this description may imply attributes that not all of them possessed, their office did carry a measure of prestige and dignity. Even though they were self-elected, 'a self-perpetuating oligarchy', they did represent the town not only in internal affairs but in its relations with the Crown.

The powers of the Corporation, administrative and judicial, were limited but real. The regulation of trade was one of these and shows how parochial the borough community was. The grant of freedom was the passport to participation in retail trade within the borough and admission to freedom was normally by seven years' apprenticeship or by birth. The Corporation jealously safeguarded the rights of the borough's own traders against 'foreigners'—which meant traders from anywhere outside Windsor. Thus in 1560 the shoemakers of Windsor petitioned the Council concerning the 'foreign Shoemakers resorting to the Town on the market days [who] make open sale of their wares, to their great hindrance, and therefore pray they may be avoided'.[8]

One of the most important powers of the Corporation was the right to return the borough's two members of Parliament. This exclusive right was challenged by the townspeople in the crucial elections to the Long Parliament in 1640. But until then this small, undemocratically chosen body of 30 citizens undemocratically chose Windsor's MPs. Not that this was done without a sense of responsibility. Sometimes a local country gentleman was chosen. Thus, at the end of Elizabeth's reign, Sir John Norreys, who held land in White Waltham and Shottesbrooke, served for Windsor. Sometimes a man closely connected with the Court was chosen. Such a one was unexpectedly named Julius Caesar, son of the Venetian physician to Queen Elizabeth. The town, however, liked to have at least one member who was someone of importance in the local community. In 1575 the Corporation had resolved 'that when the Burgesses of the parliament shall be chosen, a Townsman shall be chosen for one'.[9] Thus, a few years before this, in 1563, Richard Gallys, three times Mayor of Windsor and landlord of the Garter Inn, was chosen. Three successive Recorders or Under Stewards of Windsor, Thomas Durdent, Humphrey Newberry and Thomas Woodward, served in the Parliaments of James I and Charles I.

The Castle towered on its hill above the town. The basic plan of the Castle had not changed since the 14th century, when Edward III had extended the Castle and its walls to their present limits. The Upper Ward on the highest part of the hill contained the royal apartments, the 'pryvie lodginges'. St George's Chapel, only completed in the early part of the 16th century, was in the Lower Ward, along with the residences of the Dean and Canons and those of the Poor Knights. Between the two Wards, on its mound, was the Round Tower or Keep, a squat but formidable piece of masonry, successor to the wooden fort of the Conqueror. To the south the castle looked out over the expanse of the Forest and the Parks, with their oak woodlands, their herds of deer and some of the best hunting country in England. To the north the steep slope of the escarpment was broken by the Terrace, constructed in the time of Henry VIII and Elizabeth, with views across the Thames to Eton and the wooded hills of the Chilterns.

Windsor was only one of the royal residences. Whitehall was the most important and had something of the same status as today's Buckingham Palace. There was also St James' Palace; Henrietta Maria had her chapel here and it was here that the future Charles II was born in 1630. On the outskirts of London were Greenwich and Hampton Court. There were in addition the royal 'houses of attendance' at Richmond, Nonsuch and Oatlands.

Few years passed from the accession of James I to the outbreak of the Civil War in 1642 when the King did not spend some time at Windsor. But the sojourns were usually limited to a few days at a time. Sometimes

14

visits to Windsor were dictated by the outbreak of plague in the Metropolis. The Sovereign had the facility denied to the vast majority of his subjects that he could move on from one royal residence to another wherever conditions seemed to be safest. If the outbreak of plague in London was followed by the outbreak of plague in Windsor, he could move to Hampton Court.

The records give us vivid glimpses of this ever-present fear of pestilence. Charles had succeeded his father on the throne in March 1625 and his marriage to the French princess, Henrietta Maria, followed almost immediately. In July, when the King and the Queen were at the Castle, 'there died two of the sickness at Windsor in a house where the Queen's priests were lodged, who were presently sent to one of the towers in Hampton Court'.[10] The plague brought a halt to the chapel services in St George's and the Castle gates were locked. The King and Queen immediately left Windsor. In October, a week after a proclamation 'for avoiding all intercourse between the Court at Windsor and Hampton Court, and the cities of London and Westminster', the King 'having advertisement that the plague was in six or seven houses in Windsor resolved to go to Hampton, where he thought he would winter'.[11] In September 1636 the King was again in Windsor at a time when there was an outbreak of pestilence in London. All Londoners were ordered to be removed 'from within six miles of Windsor Castle. They are to stay the Barge of Windsor from going any more to and from London, and to give strict command that the Barge of Reading and others passing by Windsor forbear to touch or land any person there'.[12]

Windsor had two compelling attractions for James and Charles—hunting and the Garter ceremonies. James had a passion for hunting and Windsor Park and Forest had an abundance of deer and game. Charles too loved hunting, though it is impossible to picture him pursuing the deer with the nauseating blood-lust that was characteristic of his father.

The Garter ceremonies also played an important part in the life of the Court, and St George's and Windsor were the historic setting for them. As early in his reign as December 1625 Charles was at the Castle for the installation of new Knights of the Garter. The bells of the Parish Church were on this and many subsequent occasions rung at his coming.[13]

One of the happiest occasions for the King must have been in May 1638 when his eldest son, Charles, Prince of Wales, was made a Knight of the Garter. The Prince reached his eighth birthday at the end of the month and the King had taken pride in his growing family—Charles in 1630, Mary in 1631, James in 1633. Another son and two more daughters were to follow. The bells of the Parish Church were rung to celebrate every new royal birth and in 1640 a deputation from the Corporation went to the Castle with presents for Prince Charles and his brother James, now the Duke of York. The presents consisted of 'two hunters horns, tipted and adorned with silver and gold of goldsmith's work, and two fair green Taffety scarves to hang them at, richly embroidered with gold; and edged with a very great gold and silver bone lace at the ends of them, fastened to the horns with great broad ribbon'.[14]

The 1630s were the least troubled period of Charles' reign. His affection for his Queen had grown over the years and the cloud on the horizon seemed at times no bigger than a man's hand. Whether he was at Whitehall or Greenwich or Hampton Court or Windsor he found fulfilment in the intimacy of family life, in the pageantry of the Court and in the deeper satisfactions of his religious faith.

He loved St George's Chapel, not only because of its associations with the Order of the Garter of which he was the Sovereign, but because of the beauty enshrined in its architecture and craftsmanship as well as in the liturgy and the sacraments that hallowed the worship.

We have no precise knowledge of the furnishings of Windsor Castle at this time, though we get glimpses through the Commonwealth inventories of later years. Windsor did not rank high among the royal residences and, when Charles and his Court came to Windsor, many of the accessories of Court life were probably brought with them.

This of course would be especially true if the stay at Windsor was to be of short duration. Nonetheless, once installed in the Castle, the life of the Court followed an ordered routine. Charles believed in the punctilious etiquette which never allowed men to forget that he was the King. In comparison with the Court of James I, that of Charles was decorous and sober. That did not mean that there was no entertainment, but everything now had an air of culture and refinement which was lacking in his father's reign. Masques, theatrical performances, music, dancing filled the leisure hours. He enjoyed recreation too—hunting and riding in the Park, swimming and playing tennis. Dignity there was, but the King lacked the common touch. He was always conscious, as he said on the scaffold in his dying moments, that 'a subject and a sovereign are clear different things'. He held himself aloof from ordinary mortals. This was chiefly a mental attitude; but his embarrassing stammer accentuated his difficulty in communicating.

If the peaceful decade of the 1630s had been extended, Windsor might have witnessed many changes. For there are many indications that Charles had an affection for Windsor and would have devoted time and money to improving both the exterior and the interior of the Castle, so that many of the improvements brought about by his son in the 1670s would have been anticipated by some 30 years. In 1635 plans were made for re-building the banqueting house erected by Queen Elizabeth at the north-east of the Castle and for building a new wall and gateway leading into the Little Park. Elias Ashmole, the antiquary whose *Institutions, Laws and Ceremonies of the most Noble Order of the Garter* was published in 1672, says that Charles intended to enlarge the 'Tombhouse' (the present Albert Memorial Chapel) and make it 'fit and capable not only for the interment of his own royal body, but also for the bodies of his successors, Kings of England, *had not bad times drawn on*'.[15] No doubt other plans would have followed and Inigo Jones, who had created both the Banqueting House at Whitehall and the Queen's House at Greenwich, lived until 1652. The Surveyor of the Castle, to whom instructions went for carrying out the King's orders, was Sir Robert Bennett, who was later a leading Puritan in the town and one of the lay ministers appointed to officiate in the Parish Church in 1647. Some of the preliminary demolition was carried out but little of the new work materialised.

Beneath the walls of the Castle was a *puritan* town, or at least a town with strong puritan elements. This is not surprising in itself. Many of the country's towns, large and small, were puritan and supported Parliament during the Civil War. What is surprising perhaps is that Windsor was puritan in spite of the intimate relationship between Town and Crown.

How far back did Puritanism in Windsor go? It is tempting to look back as far as the 'Windsor Martyrs' of 1544, when Robert Testwood, Henry Filmer and Anthony Pierson were burned as heretics beneath the Castle walls. Clearly they held beliefs akin to those of the later Puritans, so that if it is premature to call them Puritans they certainly foreshadowed Puritanism. The views of Luther and Calvin were gaining ground and the wind of change was blowing strongly. Henry Filmer was a Windsor man, a churchwarden, Robert Testwood was a musician at St George's and Anthony Pierson a priest who 'frequented much to Windsor'. The whole story is told in vivid detail in John Foxe's *Book of Martyrs,* published in 1563. John Marbeck, the St George's musician, who himself had only been reprieved at the last moment, was still alive at the time the *Book of Martyrs* was written and gave Foxe much of his material for the Windsor story.

The burning of the Protestant Martyrs, Robert Testwood, Henry Filmer and Anthony Pierson, which took place below the Castle in 1544. From a woodcut by A. Sallaert in Foxe's Book of Martyrs.

Foxe's book was soon in every cathedral and in most parish churches in the land and, next to the *Authorised Version* of the Bible itself, exercised a profound influence on the generation before the outbreak of the Civil War in 1642. The editions of this period prominently feature Antoine Sallaert's graphic woodcut of the Windsor martyrdom. So that, even if many years had passed since the Windsor martyrs had gone to the stake, the memory of their heroism and their suffering was still very much alive.

John Martin, Vicar of Windsor from 1610 to 1633, was clearly a puritan in his views and practices. The churchwardens' accounts have many entries about fines for swearing, drunkenness and non-attendance at church. Those for 1626 include:

'Recd of John Thoringly for having persons tipling in his
house in service time   2s
Recd Dec 5 of Norton Greene by the command of Mr Mayor
for being drunk   5s
Recd of Gilbert Strowde for swearing   1s
Recd of Wright's servant for swearing   1s
Recd of Robert Sea, Rich. Nethercliff, H. Asson, Isaac
Walkers, brother Cornish his son, and Robt. Maunde for
playing at Cat in the Park meadow in service time   5s.6d

There is evidence that the inhabitants of Windsor objected to some of the entertainments in the Castle. When Ben Jonson's masque of the *Metamorphosed Gipsies* was performed before James I in 1621, a verse was introduced into the play containing the words:

'Come Windsor the town
With the Mayor and oppose.'[16]

Martin died in 1633 and was succeeded as Vicar by John Cleaver, who reversed many of his predecessor's puritan practices. Dr Goodman, the Bishop of Gloucester, in a letter to the Mayor in August 1635, said 'Hath not the Town of Windsor sometimes received a check for Puritanism; in truth I had thought and hoped that all such fancies and humours had been buried with Mr Martin, for sure I am your now Minister broacheth no such doctrine'.[17]

The entries in the churchwardens' accounts make it clear that Cleaver introduced changes. Various works are recorded in 1633 itself, including 'the railing in the communion table' and 'new paving the chancel'. In the following year more money was spent 'for beautifying and adorning the church'. Other entries refer to further items in connection with the restoration of the church, the removal of the font, the gift of two silver flagons for the communion table and the increase of the living by annexing a fellowship of Eton College 'to the Vicarage of Windsor for ever'. Scattered through the accounts from year to year are many entries with an unpuritanical ring, 'hanging the Saints Bell', 'long mats for the seat where the Godfathers kneel' and 'ix lbs of candles burnt at morning prayer'.

William Laud had become Archbishop of Canterbury in the same year that Cleaver became Vicar of Windsor and the latter's changes in the parish church reflected the practices which Laud himself approved.

How far this reversal of puritan practices met with approval in the town is another question. A controversy which arose in 1635 over the Market Cross seems to show that puritan sympathies were as strong as ever. Two years before, Dr Godfrey Goodman, who was a Canon of St George's as well as being Bishop of Gloucester, had presented an organ to the parish church, perhaps to assist the new Vicar in his attempt to restore the traditional ritual and order after the puritan regime of John Martin. In 1635, Bishop Goodman announced his intention to provide at his own expense for the restoration of the Market Cross. The Cross, first erected in 1380, stood near the junction of the four principal streets of the town: High Street, Peascod Street, Thames Street and Castle Street. It was in need of repair; the Bishop described it as 'an old cross ready to fall'. The building of the new Market House in the 1590s had perhaps made the Cross, the 'Round Market House' as it was often called, unnecessary. But the Bishop proposed not only to 'beautify and repair' the Cross, but to place a painted crucifix on its top. A contemporary description said: 'On one side there is a large statue of Christ in colours (after the Popish Garbs in foreign parts, hanging on the Cross, with this Latin inscription over it, *Jesus Nazarenus, Rex Judaeorum,* in great gilded letters); on the other side, the picture of Christ rising out of the Sepulchre, with his body half in, and half out of it. And to manifest that he is not ashamed of this scandalous work, it is thereupon engraven, that this was done at the Cost of Godfrey, Bishop of Gloucester'.

The Mayor, Francis Jones, in a letter to the Bishop made a diplomatic but pointed protest against 'the erecting of a new Crucifix where never was any before in the heart of our public market place'. The Bishop replied in a lengthy letter on the following day. This was the letter in which he referred to the town's recent reputation for puritanism quoted above. He wrote with feeling, ending with the words: 'Good Mr Mayor pardon me for this hasty scribbling which is written with a little passion'. In the course of his letter he said what he thought about the opposition to his proposal: 'But now Mr Mayor, they who have intreated you to write unto me against a new Crucifix, do you think that in their hearts and inward thoughts they do approve of any Crucifix at all'.[18]

The town nonetheless went ahead with a petition to the King, complaining of this and other acts of the Bishop. The petition was unsuccessful. The Crucifix, however, was demolished in 1643, when the Puritans were once more in the ascendancy in Windsor.

So the puritan town existed side by side with the royal Castle until in February 1642, the year of the outbreak of the Civil War, Charles left Windsor for the last time as a free man and in the following October the puritan Parliament and its puritan army took possession of the Castle.

Charles I. After Van Dyke. (NPG)

The Gathering Storm

The conflict between Parliament and King which led to the Civil War first developed menacingly in the 1620s. Five Parliaments—two in James' reign and three in Charles'—were summoned in rapid succession, only to be summarily dissolved. In 1629 Charles began the period of personal rule which lasted until 1640. This was not a tyrannical innovation. English sovereigns had often ruled without Parliament, sometimes for many years. But the five Parliaments of the 1620s had produced a new situation; Parliament had asserted its rights and the King's attempt to rule without Parliament was fraught with significance for both Church and State. Nonetheless the life of the country outwardly followed a tranquil course.

Charles could probably have maintained his personal rule but for one factor—the need for money. Even though he used the ways and means open to him, legal and illegal, to raise the money needed for the expenses of government, any abnormal expenditure could weight the scales against him. Ultimately it was to be the challenge of the Scots, a challenge which Charles had invited through his threat to their Presbyterian religion, which brought his rule without Parliament to an end.

Before the Scottish crisis reached its climax, however, the controversy over ship money arose. Kings in time of war had long exercised the right of calling upon maritime counties either to contribute ships or to pay an equivalent in cash. But now, in 1634, the demand was made in time of peace, and in the following year the tax was repeated and imposed on inland as well as maritime counties. In 1636 a third levy was announced. It was at this point that John Hampden, the Buckinghamshire squire, challenged the legality of ship money in the law courts. When the case was tried in the next year seven judges came down on the side of the King and five against. The King thus won the legal battle, but the moral victory went to Hampden and all over the country, but especially in Hampden's own county and the other counties of the Thames Valley, resistance· to the payment of ship money was widespread. In Windsor several prominent inhabitants refused to pay and their goods were distrained; others were arrested and brought before the Court of Star Chamber. William Taylor, one of the Windsor MPs chosen by the townspeople for the Long Parliament in 1640, was one of these, but 'on promise of conformity, and paying the ship-money, was discharged'. At least five persons living within the Castle resisted payment. The official record reads: 'Return having been made by the Mayor of Windsor that certain persons refuse to pay ship-money and that they living within the Castle of Windsor the collectors have no power to distrain, it was ordered that the Earl of Holland, constable of the castle, should cause assistance to be given in distraining'. The persons named were Mr Elwes, Mrs Home, Mrs Osborne and Mr Newberry, each assessed at £1, and Mr Eveley at 10s.[1]

No clearer expression of the opposition to ship-money exists than in the Petition of the Berkshire Grand Jury in July 1640. After declaring that they were 'much burdened with sundry grievances, of divers natures, deriving their authority from your majesty, but being directly contrary to your majesty's laws, established in this your kingdom', they denounce 'the illegal and insupportable charge of ship money, now the 5th year imposed as high as ever'. They go on to protest against 'the new tax of coat and conduct money, with the undue means used to inforce the payment of it, by messengers from the council table'. This tax was to cover the cost of levying men for the Scots War. The Berkshire Petition refers to 'the compelling of some freemen by imprisonment and by threatenings to take press money, and others, for fear of the like imprisonment, to forsake their places of habitation, hiding themselves in woods, whereby their families are left to be maintained by the parish, and harvest work undone for want of labourers'.[2] Such was the feeling in Berkshire a few months before the calling of the Long Parliament.

The King's increasing need for money forced him to summon Parliament. The Short Parliament, called in April 1640, immediately raised the cry of 'No taxation without redress of grievances' and was dissolved three weeks after its first meeting. But the respite for Charles was short-lived. The Scots invaded England. Newcastle had to be abandoned, and the Scots occupied all Northumberland and Durham. Charles twisted and turned in every direction. It was to no avail. A new Parliament was summoned, and held its first meeting on 3 November 1640.

The elections for the two members to represent Windsor in the Long Parliament were the most dramatic and the most important in the long history of the borough to that time. There had been no sign of any challenge to the Corporation's sole right of election for the five Parliaments of the 1620s. The choice of members for the Short Parliament does not appear to have followed any different course. One was Sir Richard Harrison, who had previously been a member for Berkshire, of which county he was also Sheriff. He was High Steward of Wokingham and lived at Hurst House and East Court Manor, Finchampstead. Sir Richard seems to fit into the category of the local country gentleman, a class which had supplied Windsor with many MPs in the past. The second was a man of considerable distinction and notoriety. Sir Arthur Ingram had sat in every Parliament from 1609. He had been Lord Mayor and MP for York, where his house was one of the most palatial in the north of England. When King Charles was at York in 1639 members of his suite stayed at Ingram's house. Sir Arthur's name was put forward for Windsor on the recommendation of the Earl of Holland, High Steward of Windsor and Constable of the Castle. Ingram chose in the event to sit for Callington in Cornwall, which he also represented in the Long Parliament until his death in 1642.

The elections for the Long Parliament were, however, contested. Sir Thomas Roe, who had served both James and Charles with distinction as Ambassador in many foreign courts including that of the 'Great Mogul in the East Indies', and Thomas Waller, Under Steward or Recorder of Windsor, were chosen by the Corporation. One interesting attempt at intervention was unsuccessful. The King's sister, Elizabeth, Queen of Bohemia, wrote from the Hague to Sir Thomas Roe, saying that she had sent 'a letter by Capt Wrenham for the Earl of Holland, desiring him to get Sir R. Cave made a burgess for Windsor. I pray Capt Wrenham come not too late'.[3] In any case the townspeople had themselves assembled at the Market Cross and made their own choice of Cornelius Holland and William Taylor. Roe and Waller were duly returned by the Corporation, but Cornelius Holland challenged the return and the Commons Committee for Privileges which determined a number of disputed elections to the Long Parliament declared in favour of the wider franchise. A new writ was issued on 10 December and the new return is dated the 16th. William Taylor had died in the meantime, but as a result of the new election his son, also William, and Cornelius Holland were chosen members.[4]

Taylor was later (27 May 1641) expelled from the House for criticising the arbitrary condemnation of Charles I's minister, the Earl of Strafford, by Act of Parliament, which he said was 'to commit murder with the Sword of Justice'. He was committed to the Tower, 'there to remain during the pleasure of the House, and shall make acknowledgement of his offence, here at the Bar, and at Windsor publicly'. On 2 June Taylor petitioned to be restored, but was refused.[5] Richard Winwood was returned in his place and so, along with Cornelius Holland, represented Windsor in the Long Parliament.

Richard Winwood was the eldest surviving son of Sir Ralph Winwood, who was for a time a Secretary of State under James I. As the owner of Ditton Park and Manor near Slough, he could be accounted a 'local man'. He supported the cause of Parliament, but was always a moderate in political matters and was one of the MPs excluded at the time of Pride's Purge in December 1648. When the Restoration came, he had no great difficulty in making his way back into public life. He was elected in 1660 by the burgesses of Windsor to the Convention Parliament which prepared the way for the return of Charles II, but was probably excluded and did not serve in the ultra-royalist Cavalier Parliament which sat from 1661 to 1679. Astonishingly, he re-appeared as a member for Windsor in the three short-lived Parliaments of 1679-81. The old controversy about who had the right to elect again raised its head and Winwood was elected by the votes of the townspeople, not the Corporation.

Richard Winwood was typical of many country gentlemen who supported Parliament during the Civil War but kept in the background after 1648. Cornelius Holland was a much more important figure. He was born on 3 March 1599, probably at Colchester, and there is good reason to believe that he was a son of Ralph, who settled in the parish of St Lawrence Pountney in London. He was educated at Merchant Taylors School and at Pembroke Hall, Cambridge. By 1626 he was a clerk in the Cofferer's office under Sir Henry Vane, to whose patronage he was deeply indebted, and by a series of promotions had by 1635 become Clerk Comptroller of the newly established Household of the Prince of Wales; in 1638 he was promoted to be Paymaster and sole Clerk of the Greencloth to the Prince. Other offices that came his way included those of Revenue Commissioner and Warden of the Tower Mint.

This record seemed to suggest that his future interest would lie in the service of the Court. Instead his course took him in the opposite direction and by 1641 he was not only a member of the Long Parliament but was committed to the extremist wing of the Parliamentary cause. There had been straws in the wind before the elections of 1640. In the previous year he had refused to subscribe to the loan for the war against the Scots. It may have been his court service that brought him to Windsor and made him known in the town; but his election by the townspeople suggests that his puritan sympathies were known and appreciated. Once in the House of Commons he remained prominent in the Parliamentary interest throughout the period of the Civil War and the years that followed and

The former Parish Church of St John the Baptist. The history of the church goes back to the 12th century and, with much re-building, it served Windsor until its demolition in 1820.

he rose to be a member of the republican Council of State after the King's execution in 1649.

Modern scholars warn against reading too much into the elections for the Long Parliament. This is true of the Windsor elections as of many others. There were no political parties. There was no vote by ballot, either open or secret. There was no clear appreciation of the great constitutional issues at stake. Although there was deep resentment at taxes like ship-money, local issues often counted for more than national ones. Antagonism towards the municipal oligarchy probably played a part as well.

Nonetheless the townspeople of Windsor did successfully challenge the Corporation's monopoly of electoral privilege. The Mayor and the brethren of the Corporation sat in the Guildhall and made their return of two members to sit in Parliament. The townspeople met at the Market Cross and declared their preference by voices or by hands—'the cry and the view'. There were no such things as poll-books or electoral registers. We know, however, that the indenture for the return of Cornelius Holland and William Taylor in December 1640 was attested by the Mayor, Bailiffs and 40 citizens 'together with divers other the Burgesses and inhabitants of the said Borough'.[6] That for the return of Richard Winwood at the by-election in the summer of 1641 was attested by no fewer than 179 persons 'being the major part of the Burgesses and Inhabitants'.[7]

Whatever reservations may be made, the results of the elections of 1640 were far-reaching. The Long Parliament met in November 1640. In the next year a constitutional revolution was carried through. The Courts of Star Chamber and High Commission were abolished. Ship-money and a wide range of extra-parliamentary methods of raising money were declared illegal. Strafford was executed and Laud imprisoned. The Triennial Act was passed to ensure the regular summoning of Parliament, and, with the experience in mind of the Parliaments of the 1620s and of the Short Parliament of 1640 itself, an Act was forced upon the King that the Long Parliament could not be dissolved without its own consent.

With many of these measures there was virtual unanimity. It was not until the summer of 1641 that a cleavage began to develop between the radical and moderate factions in Parliament, both in the Commons and in the Lords. The cleavage came over two issues in particular: one was the future of the bishops; the second was the control of the militia, a question made urgent by the outbreak of rebellion in Ireland.

In the midst of the controversies, in August 1641 the King left London for Scotland and, although fears of his intentions were profound, he was not prevented from making his journey.

What was happening in Windsor during the last year before the outbreak of the Civil War in August 1642? The readiness with which

Windsor rallied to the support of Parliament when the war came suggests that the town's sympathies were always strongly with the Parliamentary cause. The uncertainties of the times are reflected in three of our main local sources. There are no churchwardens' accounts entered for the year 1641-42, although there are three blank pages in the book, evidently for their insertion. Similar gaps and deficiencies occur in the registers of baptisms, marriages and burials as the period of the Civil War is approached. The chamberlains' accounts continue, but after Michaelmas 1640 there is a falling off, both in the regularity of the entries, and in the amount of the receipts.

Lawlessness was on the increase. Windsor Park and Forest with their deer and their game had always been a temptation to poachers. In the unsettled period before the Civil War the King had few opportunities for hunting and hawking. Moreover, the revival and enforcement of the forest laws in the 1630s helped to protect the deer. The Berkshire Grand Jury Petition of 1640 referred to 'the unmeasurable increase of deer, which if they shall go on for a few more years will leave neither food nor room for any other creature in the forest'.[8]

The royal officer responsible as Constable for the maintenance of law and order in the Park and Forest was the Earl of Holland. Appointed Constable in 1637, when he was a courtier in favour with the King, at the outbreak of the Civil War he came down on the Parliamentary side. Although he belonged to the peace party that worked for a negotiated settlement with the King, he gave general support to the Parliamentary cause during the War. In 1648, however, he took the Royalist side in the Second Civil War, but was taken prisoner, tried, condemned to death and executed in March 1649. For a time after his capture he was confined in the Castle where, as the Earl of Clarendon, the Royalist historian, says 'notwithstanding that he was Constable of it, he was kept prisoner with great strictness'. 'A fine gentleman in good times' is Clarendon's pointed judgment of him.[9]

His task at Windsor was certainly beyond his capacity. When the King was in Scotland in the autumn of 1641, organised bands of poachers killed and carried off deer, threatened murder and the burning of houses, barns and haystacks. The House of Commons, on 8 September 1641, directed the Solicitor-General and four other MPs to initiate action to deal with the troubles.[10] The disturbances continued, however, and on 18 February 1642 the Earl of Holland informed the Lords 'of the great destruction and killing of His Majesty's deer in the Forest of Windsor, especially in the New Lodge, where the People of the Country, in riotous and tumultuous manner, have lately killed a hundred of His Majesty's Fallow Deer, and besides Red Deer, and do threaten to pull down the Pales about the said Lodge'.[11] Four months later, in June, Holland ordered Ralph Maddison, Keeper of the Walks of Battle and Easthampstead in Windsor Forest to search 'for greyhounds, dogs, hand-guns, crossbows, nets, traps and other engines used to kill and destroy the deer'.[12] A few of the intruders were caught. We know some of their names: Henry Bannister of Wokingham, Aminadab Harrison and George Godfrey of Easthampstead, Richard Hayworth, Richard Gason of Warfield. Some were 'forthwith sent from Constable to Constable, unto the House of Correction in the County of Berks, there to be kept to work'. Others were committed to Newgate.[13]

In November 1641 the Grand Remonstrance, with its long catalogue of the King's misdeeds, was placed before the Commons by John Pym. On the night of the 22nd the Commons sat late and, in the flickering light of candles, the debate continued until 1am. When the House divided, 159 voted for the Remonstrance and 148 against. The King's opponents had gained their greatest victory.

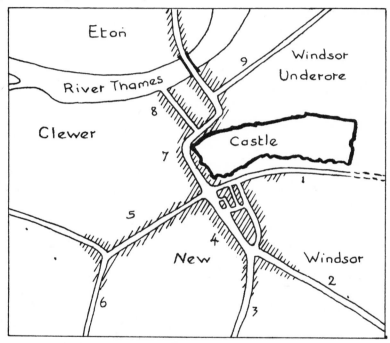

Seventeenth century Windsor. Key (with modern names in brackets): 1. Castle Street (Castle Hill) 2. Moor Street (Park Street) 3. Sheet Street 4. High Street 5. Peascod Street 6. Spital Street (St Leonards Road) 7. Bridge Street (Thames Street) 8. Bereman Street (River Street) 9. Datchet Lane (Datchet Road)

The King had left Edinburgh on the 18th and by the day of the crucial debate was within two days' ride of London. On the morning of the 25th he entered the City to receive the traditional welcome given to a Sovereign returning to his capital. Throughout December he was at Whitehall, anxiously watching the fluctuating situation. At the beginning of January he decided to strike against the five leading members of the

Commons. But the coup miscarried and the attempt to arrest Pym and his colleagues in the House of Commons itself on the 4th failed.

This defeat spelt disaster for the King. London was angry and hostile. The Trained Bands had been mobilised and were standing to arms. Any day they might march on Whitehall, where an irresolute Charles still lingered.

On the evening of the 10th, however, he left Whitehall, not to return until the time of his execution. The coaches carrying the Royal Family to Hampton Court had to make their way through threatening crowds. When the King and Queen reached their destination they found that no apartments had been prepared for them and they had to bed down for the night with their children in a single room.

The next day or the day after (the accounts differ) they moved on to Windsor, where the King might be 'more secure from any popular attempt than he could be in the rebellious capital'.[14] On 14 January the Commons heard that the King was concentrating troops at Windsor. Parliament protested against this: 'it causeth much wonder at this time, a Parliament sitting, that such forces should be levied, and all at Peace'. Some sudden action on the King's side was evidently feared, but the King remained quietly at Windsor, receiving messages and deputations from Parliament.

On the 20th Charles wrote to Parliament from Windsor, declaring that he would 'exceed the great examples of the most indulgent princes' in coming to an agreement with them and calling heaven to witness that he had never designed anything against them.[15] These brave but disingenuous words could not disguise the seriousness of his situation. Even at this time he was, according to Clarendon, 'fallen in ten days from a height of greatness that his enemies feared, to such a lowness, that his own servants durst hardly avow the waiting on him'. 'Every corner', continues Clarendon, 'was possessed by diligent spies upon their master and mistress'. The same authority says that when the King and Queen were at Windsor they were reduced to comparative want, the Queen being 'compelled to coin or sell her chamber plate, for the supply of her most necessary occasions, there being no money in the exchequer, or in the power of the ministers of the revenue; the officers of the customs, out of which the allowance for the weekly support of their majesties' household had been made, being enjoined by the House of Commons not to issue out any money, without their particular approbation'.[16]

On 2 February some members appointed by both Houses of Parliament attended the King at Windsor, with a petition to place the Tower of London and all other forts, and the militia of the kingdom, in the hands of such persons as should be recommended to His Majesty by both Houses of Parliament. The King determined not to assent to this request, but prevaricated because he feared further demands.[17]

Even at Windsor there were still fears for the security of the King and Queen. There were rumours that a thousand citizens were coming from London to present a petition to the King at Windsor; Clarendon speaks of 'the tumults which might easily be brought to Windsor from Westminster'.[18] Charles was especially concerned for the safety of the Queen and thought it best that she should take refuge in Holland. So, on 9 February, the King left Windsor with the Queen and, after parting from her at Dover on the 23rd, he returned to Greenwich where he was joined by the Prince of Wales. From Greenwich the King went to Theobalds in Hertfordshire, thence to Newmarket and subsequently to York.[19]

This last sojourn at Windsor, in circumstances as cheerless as they were foreboding, was in stark contrast to earlier visits, with days filled with hunting in the Park, the pageantry of Court life, the appreciation of music and the arts and the enjoyment of family life. All the pleasures of life at Windsor were now only memories. Twice more, before his execution, Charles came to Windsor, once in July 1647 and, for the last time, in December 1648, but on both occasions he was under restraint, in every respect that mattered a prisoner.

Henrietta Maria. After Van Dyke. (NPG)

29

Henry Rich, Earl of Holland, was constable of Windsor Castle at the outbreak of the Civil War. After Van Dyke. (NPG)

The Storm Breaks

The King raised his standard at Nottingham on 22 August 1642, but preparations for the coming conflict had already been going on for several months.

Windsor supported the Parliamentary cause from the outset. As early as 13 July, the House of Commons ordered 'the payment of £150 to the Town of Windsor, advanced and lent by them, out of the monies collected at Windsor, upon the Bill of £400,000, as was made for Bucks'.[1] On 16 September it was ordered ' that Mr Holland shall have liberty to send down ten Muskets and their Equipage to the Town of Windsor, for the service of that Town'—not a very generous allocation, one would have thought, but perhaps intended as a token when arms and ammunition were still in short supply.[2]

It was only a matter of weeks before the war approached Windsor. The battle of Edgehill, fought south of Warwick on 23 October, did not lead to a decisive victory for either side but left the road to London open to the King. A swift advance might have brought success, but the opportunity was missed, never to recur. Banbury was captured on the 27th. On the 29th the King entered Oxford. It was nearly a week later, on 4 November, that he reached Reading.

In the meantime Parliament had acted over Windsor. The Castle was there for the taking. In later days fortresses like the Tower of London and Windsor Castle would have been garrisoned; but at the beginning of the Civil War the King had no standing army at his disposal and he could not therefore take effective measures to keep command of such strongholds. Nonetheless, as the Royalist forces reached the Thames Valley, speed of action was essential. Both King and Parliament recognised the importance of the Castle 'being a place of greatest strength in this part of the kingdom, by reason of the height and strength, the country lying under it so that the Castle can command it round about'.[3]

As early as 17 October the House of Commons had agreed 'that it be recommended to the Committee for the Defence of the Kingdom, to take some especial care of Windsor Castle'.[4] On the 28th Parliamentary forces occupied the Castle and put it in a state of defence. From all the surrounding counties, Middlesex, Buckinghamshire, Berkshire, Surrey, Hampshire, troops of dragoons, militiamen and volunteers were raised and concentrated on Windsor. 'Others', the account continues, 'are in their march towards Windsor, where being arrived, they intend to fortify themselves, and to make out-workers, so that the Cavaliers have lost their labour'.[5]

The Parliamentary commander who now also became Governor of the Castle was Col John Venn. Venn remained as Governor until June 1645 and was one of the dominating figures in all that went on in Windsor during the Civil War. Like Cromwell himself, he was a notable example of the civilian turned soldier. His background was that of a City merchant. He became one of London's MPs in the Long Parliament and was 'ceaselessly industrious' in the Parliamentary cause, both in and out of Parliament. He worked hard to consolidate puritan control over the City government and attained renown for his ability to mobilise public opinion in the City. He was prominent in the opposition to Charles I's entry into London and the City's welcome to the King on his return from Scotland in November 1641.

As early as 1636 Venn became a 'captain serjeant major' in the Artillery Company and by the beginning of 1642 he was playing an important part in working out plans for the defence of the City. The Trained Bands were increased, equipped and placed under the command of Major-General Philip Skippon, a bible-and-sword soldier who had seen service on the Continent. From that time Parliament had the backing not only of the City government but of an effectively organised armed force, the City Trained Bands. These were to play a vital part in halting the King's advance on London in November 1642.

Shortly after the outbreak of the Civil War, Venn appears as a colonel of foot in the Parliamentary army. He took part in the fight at Worcester on 23 September and was in command of a party of horse employed in guarding the passages of the Severn.

It is easy to understand why John Venn was appointed Governor of Windsor Castle when the need arose. He had acquired a formidable reputation as an antagonist of the King. The Royalists hated him and he is frequently execrated in their newspapers and letters for his harshness, fanaticism and intolerance. In June 1642 he was one of the six MPs who, together with those charged with treason, were exempted from the King's pardon. In the 'peace negotiations' in December 1642 Charles stipulated that several citizens were to be surrendered and tried for high treason; Venn was one of these.[6]

When the First Civil War ended in 1646, he returned to London and was an energetic member of the army committee of the House of Commons. He took a full share in the trial of the King and signed the death warrant. He seemed destined to be one of the leading figures in the new republic, but he was now over 60 and died in June 1650.

Just over a week after Venn had taken over his duties at Windsor in October 1642, the Royalists under Prince Rupert attacked the Castle on 7 November. Venn's toughness and military ability proved more than a match for the dash and gallantry of the Prince. The contemporary

accounts of the conflict are confusing. The town itself may even have
been taken for a brief period—unlike Oxford, Windsor town had no
fortifications. The Castle itself, however, was far too strong for Rupert's
slender resources. His 'five pieces of Ordnance', firing from the grounds
of Eton College, did considerable damage in the town. A contemporary
pamphlet, *Joyful Tidings from Windsor,* reported: 'As for the town, that
is mightily battered and ruined, and the inhabitants very much damnified.
All which stood well-affected to the Parliament went into the castle and

Prince Rupert, Royalist cavalry commander; nephew of
Charles I. Attributed to G. Honthurst c1641-2. (NPG)

are safe'. Others fled into the woods. The artillery bombardment continued for seven hours, but the walls of the Castle suffered very little damage. Venn distinguished himself in the fighting. 'Col Venn', says the same contemporary account 'behaved himself very bravely, to the wonder and amazement of the beholders'. This makes it seem likely that Venn led a sortie from the Castle. Eventually Rupert drew off. His Cavaliers told him (according to the colourful and not altogether impartial narrative of the Parliamentarian pamphleteer) that 'they would willingly attend him to fight against men but not against stone walls, rocks and inaccessible places, where a hundred men might keep out ten thousand, all valour being useless, and therefore desired the Prince that he would rise thence, and depart into other places where they might do the Cause better service'.[7]

The King meanwhile continued his advance towards London. Again he was too slow and too late. Essex, the Parliamentary commander, had reached London first. He had made his way back after Edgehill by a route well to the north of the Royalists and was at the capital by 7 November—the day that Rupert made his attack on Windsor. By the 11th Charles was only at Colnbrook, some three miles to the east of Windsor. Parliament, however, was frightened by the approach of the Royalist forces and sent commissioners to Colnbrook to ask the King to appoint some convenient place for a Conference. Charles seized the opportunity of suggesting Windsor Castle as suitable, provided the Parliamentary forces there were first removed.[8] Clarendon believed that 'if the King had, as soon as the messengers returned to London, retired with his army to Reading, and there expected the Parliament's answer, they would immediately have withdrawn their garrison from Windsor, and delivered that castle to his majesty for his accommodation to have treated in'. Clarendon, however, expressed his doubts 'whether they [the peace party] would have been able to have prevailed that so considerable a strength, in so considerable a place, should have been quit, whilst there was only hope of a peace'.[9]

In the event Charles moved not backwards to Reading but forwards to Brentford. Here the advance of the Royalists was barred by Essex's regiments and the London Trained Bands. Only a few miles away were Westminster and London. For a little while it looked as if the issue would be settled by the sword rather than by the pen. But there was no battle. The King's forces retreated in face of Essex's superiority of man-power and by 19 November they were back at Reading. There he rejected Parliament's overtures and another opportunity had gone. Parliament, commented Clarendon, 'declared the King had no mind to peace; and therefore laid aside all further debate to that purpose, and ordered their general to move to Windsor with the army, to be so much nearer the King's forces'.[12] In the next few days Essex accordingly transferred his headquarters to Windsor. Before the end of the month the King, leaving a garrison of 3000 at Reading, returned to Oxford, where he settled his army into winter quarters.

Windsor Castle remained a Parliamentary stronghold for the whole of the Civil War. For much of the War it was the actual headquarters of the main Parliamentary army. Forty miles away at Oxford were the Royalist headquarters. In between the two was a no man's land which was frequently the scene of clashes between the forces of the two opposing sides.

At first Clarendon was able to boast that the King had the whole of Oxfordshire in his power, and 'all Berkshire but that barren division about Windsor'.[11] In April 1643, however, as the new campaigning season opened, the Earl of Essex marched from Windsor towards Reading with his whole army, consisting of about 16,000 foot and more than 3,000 horse. Reading, commanding one of the most important routes through the Chilterns, was of vital strategic importance to the Royalists, but it was weakly defended and surrendered to Essex after a short siege. The approaches to Oxford were still covered by garrisons at Wallingford and Abingdon, but the threat to the Royalist headquarters was now much greater. At one time Essex reached Wheatley and Islip, only a few miles from Oxford, and had outposts in Cowley and Headington, so that Clarendon now had to comment that Essex 'brought those adjacent counties entirely under the obedience of the Parliament, which would at least have kept themselves neutral'.[12] Berkshire in particular suffered from its position. 'We are exposed', said a Berkshire petition, 'as it were in the very middest, betwixt both armies'.[13] The Royalists assessed the county at £1400 per week; Parliament also not only levied its own taxes and fines but seized and administered the estates of many Royalists.

Both armies foraged far and wide over the countryside and requisitioned what supplies they required. Rupert's forays carried him far into the Chilterns, at times threatening the approaches to London. In one of these forays, in the summer of 1643, at Chalgrove Field near Watlington, John Hampden received the wound from which he died a few days later. No further attack on Windsor took place, but the threat was always present. Venn was never able to relax.

Within the Castle, however, Venn's word was law. The Royalist Bruno Ryves who at the Restoration became Dean of Windsor wrote of him that he 'doth assume to himself the propriety of his Sovereign's house, dating his letters to his wife *from our Castle at Windsor*'.[14] When the Earl of Essex moved the headquarters of his Parliamentary army to Windsor at the end of 1642, he established himself in the Round Tower. Clearly there was no love lost between Essex and Venn. Essex was an aristocrat, son of Elizabeth's favourite, professional soldier, anxious for reconciliation with the King. Such a man could hardly have seen eye to eye with Venn. John Birkenhead, the editor of the Royalist journal *Mercurius Aulicus,* alleged that 'the Earl of Essex (who hath a long time had a mind to be master of Windsor Castle but could never yet effect his purpose) did, not long since, cause a muster to be made of all Venn's regiment in the park; and in the meantime sent Sir Edward Peitow to enter the castle with 60 firelocks under the pretence of bringing some timber for the use of the artillery. But Venn had ordered his matters so that the gates should not be opened to him, nor he suffered to enter'.[15] The source may be suspect, but the allegation has a certain ring of authenticity about it.

Venn's responsibilities were increased by the confinement in the Castle of Royalist prisoners, many of them officers of distinguished rank. The first to come to Windsor—there were 55 of them—had been taken prisoner in the very first months of the war. They included three Sheriffs—Edmund Fortescue from Devon, Francis Dodington from Somerset and Edward Ford from Sussex. They had been taken first to London, where Lambeth Palace and other town residences of some of the bishops and the Royalist nobility were used. The security in London, however, was imperfect and escapes took place. So at the beginning of 1643 they were sent to Windsor to be there under the custody of Col John Venn, 'who will look a little better to them than only a few negligent persons have done'.[16] Even so Windsor was considered 'not so well fitted for the safe keeping of them as is requisite, the quality of the persons considered' and the House of Commons made an allowance for the improvement of their accommodation and laid down the conditions for their confinement. Provided they were willing to pay, they could be conveyed to Windsor in coaches and at the Castle they might have beds and other necessaries at their own charge. Each prisoner was to make a weekly payment for his accommodation. They were strictly confined to the Castle, were not allowed to speak to visitors and all their letters were censored.[17]

In spite of the last regulation we do have letters that give us vivid descriptions of the prisoners' lives, especially those of Thomas Knyvett, written in 1643 'from our Pallas at Windsor Castle'. Cromwell had nipped in the bud a Royalist rising in East Anglia and Knyvett was one of those captured. He and his companions—there may have been as many as 30 sent first to Cambridge and then to Windsor—were lodged in the houses of the Poor Knights. 'Poor men', wrote Knyvett to his wife Katherine, 'they have turned them out and put us in, and ere long we shall be as poor as they'. They had to endure some discomforts. 'I was forced', he says, 'to leave all my clothes at Cambridge, so I fear I shall be lousy before I get any change; but 'tis all our cases'. He does not complain overmuch, however. 'We are now become housekeepers, and got good things about us; for our bodies we shall do reasonably well. And for our souls God hath so provided for us as we never wanted a divine among us since our restraint. Dr Young, a prebend of Norwich, is our chaplain; our fellow prisoner, a patient, quiet, sober man. We had the liberty to go to church, forenoon and afternoon, here in the Castle, where we heard wonderful sermons.' Knyvett was not at Windsor very long. He had only been taken prisoner at Lowestoft in March 1643. By July he had been removed from Windsor to London.[18]

The Castle was strongly fortified and straitly guarded. It was, however, never only a prison; it was used for many purposes and there must have been much coming and going, so that complete security was not possible. It is not altogether surprising that there were escapes. All the three Sheriffs mentioned escaped, each after only a short period of detention.

ABOVE: Sir Edmund Fortescue's Shield and Motto. Carving in the Castle, where he was a prisoner in 1643. (By gracious permission of Her Majesty the Queen) BELOW: Col R. Powell's Shield. Prisoner in the Castle 1648. (By gracious permission of Her Majesty the Queen)

Some of the prisoners left behind them memorials of their captivity in the shape of carvings of names and armorial bearings on the walls of the prison chamber over the Norman Gateway and elsewhere. Some are merely scratched coats of arms, but some are executed with industry and considerable skill. Of outstanding interest is Sir Edmund Fortescue's shield and motto, 'Forte Scutum Salus Ducum' *(A strong shield the leader's safeguard)* and the defiant 'Pour le Roy C'. The armorial bearings of Sir Francis Dodington and Major-General Laugharne are also remarkably fine pieces of workmanship. It is strange indeed that, when the Puritan occupation of the Castle is so remote and half-forgotten, these carvings should remain as a poignant reminder of those tragic years.

East Berkshire. Section of Christopher Saxton's map of Berkshire, 1607.

38

Fortunes Of War

One of the most dramatic developments which occurred in Windsor during the early part of the Civil War was the ejection of the Dean and Canons from St George's Chapel in 1643.

Built in the last decades before the Reformation, the new St George's had taken the place of the earlier chapel built by Edward III in the 14th century, so that by the time of Charles I there had been a continuity of worship extending over three centuries. Throughout that time the Chapel had been intimately associated with the Monarchy and the Order of the Garter. It was one of the richest ecclesiastical foundations in England and its wealth was reflected not only in the magnificence of the building itself but in all the accessories, the plate, the ornaments, the furnishings, the vestments, the ceremonial, which could enrich the services and bring additional splendour to all that went on within the Chapel. Bishop Goodman remembered that God was 'continually served like a God with the greatest magnificence; we had there all the means of devotion, as music and outward ceremonies'.[1] Then, with the outbreak of the Civil War, St George's came into the hands of men to whom the high dignity of the liturgical ritual and the pageantry of the Garter ceremonies were things not of God but of Satan.

In the years before the war two famous brothers had followed each other as Deans of Windsor. Matthew Wren was Dean from 1627 to 1635, when he became Bishop first of Norwich and then of Ely. His younger brother, Christopher Wren, father of an even more famous son, took his place and remained as Dean until his ejection in 1643. Both Matthew and Christopher were intransigent enemies of Puritanism.

The Dean and Chapter of St George's were distinguished *and* Royalist. Among the twelve canons was Godfrey Goodman, Bishop of Gloucester, whose activities in Windsor were so resented by the Puritans. Another Canon was Vice-Provost of Eton and three were Fellows of the College. Four were Royal Chaplains, most had been Fellows of Oxford and Cambridge colleges and one had been Regius Professor of Greek.

The expulsion of the Dean and Canons did not take place immediately after the occupation of the Castle by Parliamentary forces in October 1642, though it was not long delayed. Dr Wren did what he could to save some of the most precious possessions of the Chapel. He refused to give up the keys of the Chapel treasury and a certain Capt Fogg had to burst open the door to gain entrance. His attempt to save the diamond-studded Garter which had belonged to Gustavus Adolphus of Sweden by burying it under the floor of the treasury chamber was at first successful, for it took three years for the puritan authorities to discover the secret of its hiding place. Wren seems to have been most successful in protecting some of the documentary records, in particular the three Register Books of the Order. The first of these was the so-called Black Book, bound in black leather, beautifully illuminated and covering the ceremonies and installations in the reigns of Henry VIII and Edward VI. The Blue Book contained a delightful miniature of the young Queen Elizabeth, and the Red Book continued the records from 1553 to 1636. These were treasures indeed and were preserved by Dean Wren until his death just before the Restoration. They then passed into the custody of his son and were returned by him to Dr Bruno Ryves, the new Dean.

However, the plate and ornaments of the Chapel were systematically plundered. As Elias Ashmole quaintly put it, 'her inside was very much abused by the Saints of those times'. The Lords gave a general directive to Col Venn 'to take care that there be no disorders and disturbances made in the Chapel at Windsor; and that the Evidences, Registers, Monuments there, and all things that belong to the Order of the Garter, may be preserved without any defacings'.[2] The Commons apparently took a different view for they ordered Venn to 'put the ordinance for removal of scandalous monuments and pictures in execution in the several churches and chapels of Windsor and Eton'. As with St Paul's Cathedral all monuments, pictures and 'all such matters as are justly offensive to godly men' were to be removed.[3] Venn needed little encouragement and a thorough plunder of the ornaments and furnishings of the Chapel took place. One of the historic relics which was seized was the coat of mail and surcoat of Edward IV. The lectern, font and candalabra went; so also did two brass statues (probably the Virgin and St George) and even 'thirteen seats of the Poor Knights, lined with scarlet'.

The Dean and Canons were finally expelled following a Commons Ordinance of April 1643. They had petitioned Parliament to be left undisturbed as they did not bear arms, and the Lords directed the Governor to permit them 'to live in their own houses so long as they live inoffensively, and conform themselves to those orders as are fit for the quiet and secure preservation of that Castle'.[4] Again, the Lords and Commons appeared to be in conflict. Venn, not surprisingly, chose to obey the Commons rather than the Lords. He was the last man to want a nest of Royalists in the castle under his charge and he decided that they must go. By May they were leaving their homes and petitioning 'that they may have liberty to carry forth all their goods, utensils, household stuffs and books to their several abodes, and that an order might be made for their safe conveying and quiet enjoying of the same, they always submitting themselves to authority'. The Lords acceded to the request and a letter was sent to Col Venn to that effect, but at the same time to see that their belongings were searched before they were carried away from Windsor.[5]

The Poor Knights, on the other hand, were allowed to remain, but in the absence of the Dean and Canons to administer the funds, their pay was soon in arrears and they found themselves in considerable distress.

The War cast long shadows over the town itself. The presence of so many troops must have had a far-reaching impact. We catch a fleeting but vivid glimpse of the disruption of normal life, when the entries in the parish registers of baptisms, marriages and burials cease abruptly, and the clerk simply records, 'This Book was neglected in the unhappy wars betwixt the King and Parliament'. The town's government continued to function. The mayors come and go and when Hercules Trew 'obstinately refused' to take the oath of office in 1643, the Corporation threatened him with legal action for 'such an affront to the Town'.[6] The Chamberlain's accounts make it clear that the Brethren nonetheless met and incurred the expense of 10s 4d 'for bread beer and wine on the day Mr Mayor should have taken his oath at the Town Hall'. It is also recorded that Thomas Browne and Thomas Durdent refused to accept election as Brethren of the Corporation. If these refusals were political there is no evidence to show it. Hercules Trew at least was almost certainly a member of the Corporation until his death in 1655. The Chamberlain's accounts, which provide so many glimpses of the activities of the Corporation, continue through the war and until 1647.

The town must have been subject to the authority of the Castle to a greater degree than had ever been true in the time of the King. Although all the evidence suggests that Windsor supported the Parliamentary cause, the town's loyalty would sometimes have been subjected to considerable strain. The Chamberlain's accounts make it clear that there were frequent meetings between representatives of the town and Col Venn or his officers. These accounts not unnaturally are more concerned with the expenses of the hospitality provided by the Mayor than with the subjects of discussion. 'Paid for a quart of sack Mr Mayor and Mr Starkey gave the Lieutenant Colonel 1s. 2d' is a typical entry. There is one specific item where 4s 5d was 'spent at the White Hart by Mr Mayor, Mr Starkey, Mr Day and Wycks with Lieutenant Colonel when they met concerning the Bulwarks'. An entry for 14 February 1645 reads: 'paid at the White Hart when Mr Mayor, Mr Day, Mr Starkey, Mr Eyres, Mr Mills and others with Castle Captains about a petition concerning soldiers' pay . . . 6s 3d'.

There were other demands on the Corporation purse. In the very first year of the war a sum of £6 was 'laid out for laying down the bridge by Colonel Venn's appointment', an entry which seems to suggest major repairs. Another item is of £1 'lent to the Constables John Fish and Richard Plumridge by Mr Mayor's discretion towards the relief of sick distressed Soldiers and towards the burying of dead Soldiers'.

Billeting laid an almost intolerable burden on the town. The numerous inns had to supply a large share of the accommodation required, and many towns and villages in the district had to take their quota. The parishioners of Harlington, between Windsor and London, for example, protested in July 1643: 'All last winter we were charged with billeting of soldiers, both horse and foot, to our exceeding great hindrance and loss; and now upon the Lord General [Essex] coming to Windsor, the horse troop belonging to the Earl of Bedford is returned upon us again, to be billeted as formerly; so that we are no way able to do what we would in this case, for we shall be very hardly able to subsist, especially if they shall continue any time with us'.[7] The pressure on Windsor itself was intense. With its population of perhaps 1,500 or less, the number of houses probably did not exceed 300 and these were often overcrowded, even without the addition of soldiers.

Householders were obliged to provide food and lodging for a certain number of soldiers at a fixed rate. This food and lodging were not provided gratis, but payment was deferred and, however well-intentioned the authorities, the money was often not forthcoming. The only satisfactory system would have been to pay the soldiers regularly and require them to defray the cost of their food and lodging. Yet the soldiers' pay was always in arrears, so that the method of quartering was based on billets or tickets presented for payment later.

The abuses to which the system of 'free quarter' was open were many. The needs of the soldiers created artificial shortages of food and of many of the necessities of life. The prices of bread and other commodities mounted. The soldiers were often packed into stuffy garrets or, if they were not, then the resident family had to make do with accommodation the soldiers did not require. Sickness was a part of life; in the wet and hot summer of 1643 pestilence was widespread. The Royalist forces at Oxford suffered. So too did the Parliamentary army in the Thames Valley and it is unlikely that Windsor escaped.

However strict the discipline, the presence of the soldiers was an unwanted intrusion in many homes. Many of the soldiers were doubtless godly Puritans—but not all, and petty thefts, quarrelsome behaviour and drunkenness were certainly not unknown. Many of the householders too were godly Puritans—but not all; some were Royalists, many were indifferent, so that the stress and strain of daily life in Windsor during the Civil War years was, for many of the townspeople, unbearable. Within a few months of the Restoration the innkeepers and victuallers petitioned for an end to the 'ruinous incumbrance' of quartering.

There was one sphere open to both townsmen and soldiers. Authority in the Park and Forest had broken down with the outbreak of war. Even before the war poaching and violence had increased. The Journals of the House of Lords record many instances of trouble in both the Great and the Little Park during the war. It might seem extraordinary that in years like 1643, 1644 and 1645, when the country was rent by civil war, the noble Lords—and by that time the Royalists had departed and left a rump of Parliamentary peers—should have found time to concern themselves with such matters. However, they described how three men from Staines came into the Great Park with three greyhounds and coursed the whole herd of deer. When the Keeper, Thomas Shemonds, and his men tried to stop them, they were attacked.[8] There are several further records of local men engaged in unlawful activity in the Park, in quest of venison rather than sport. It was the soldiers, however, who created the greatest havoc. In 1643 the soldiers quartered at Windsor committed 'sad depredations' in the Great Park. In the following year Essex's men destroyed all the deer (about 500) in the Little Park and burnt up all the pales. In the course of the wars nearly all the deer in the Great Park were wiped out, and one of the keepers was killed by a trooper.[9]

The Parliamentary garrison remained at Windsor, although as soon as the danger of an attack on the Castle receded, demands began for the reduction or even the disbanding of the garrison. The shortage both of military stores and of money to pay the soldiers accentuated the pressure. The chief opposition to the weakening of the Windsor garrison came from London, which was not convinced that all danger had passed.[10] Col Venn, as one of London's MPs, certainly gave his support to this view.

The demands took on a new urgency in 1644. By this time the Scots had entered the war on the side of Parliament and there seemed less likelihood of major campaigning in the south-east. In April the House of Commons passed a resolution that the garrison should be disbanded with a month's pay. The City successfully petitioned against this.[11] In October the House resolved that the garrison should be reduced to 200 men, in addition to officers. Arrears of pay were mounting and there was an actual mutiny of the garrison in the following month. The Governor was threatened with violence and the Commons decided to take speedy measures for the safety of the Castle, 'the House being very sensible of the present and imminent danger that place lies in'. Three hundred men of the trained bands of Middlesex were immediately sent to the Castle and a sum of £100 a week for a fortnight was allocated for their needs. At the same time certain officers of the garrison were cashiered.[12]

The soldiers at Windsor were always in arrears of pay. This was as much behind the attempts to reduce the garrison as any other factor. Where to get the money from was a problem to which Parliament never found the answer, though every possible avenue was explored. The maintenance of Col Venn's regiment of foot, exclusive of horse and artillery, was upwards of £3,000 a month.[13]

There were also the constant problems of keeping the garrison supplied with food and equipped with arms and ammunition. There is a reference, for example, on 26 September 1643 to 'the payment of wheat and other provision unto the Castle of Windsor' and places are mentioned as far away as Hurley and Knowl Hill, between Maidenhead and Reading.[14] Both sides requisitioned supplies from the districts in which troops were stationed, under promise of future payment—often an uncertain prospect. On military supplies a particularly interesting order of the Commons dated 9 August 1643 instructs Lt-Col Rowe to deliver to Col Venn '50 barrels of powder, out of the store remaining in his hand that came on the Danish ship, 300 swords and 200 muskets, with rests and bolts'.[15]

Not only was there the problem of keeping the Windsor garrison itself adequately supplied; the Castle served as a supply base for the Parliamentary armies operating between Windsor and Oxford. Essex was requested to provide an escort of horse for '20 cart-loads of ammunition and provisions' to be conveyed from Windsor to Reading. Military supplies were also sent to Reading by river, although there was some fear that Royalist forces 'which have been lately about Henley' might offer a threat. On another occasion five tons of match and spades, shovels, crows and pickaxes were sent from Windsor to Abingdon.[16]

In 1644 there are repeated references to 'the Windsor regiment'. It was included in the forces under the command of Major-General R. Browne, which in turn were a part of the army of the Earl of Essex. The regiment included a minister, surgeons, quarter-master, marshal and commissary and served both at Reading and Abingdon.[17] Recruits for the Castle garrison were on occasion drawn from 'the well affected in Windsor'.[18]

Throughout the Civil War the Parliamentary armies based on Windsor came and went as the exigencies of the war required. Essex, as we have seen, advanced from Windsor in April 1643 and captured Reading. In the late summer he was campaigning in the west, where he raised the siege of Gloucester at the beginning of September. He commanded the Parliamentary army at the first battle of Newbury on 20 September. In October, when Rupert took Bedford, Essex moved his headquarters from Windsor to St Albans to guard against a Royalist advance towards London. He returned to Windsor in December and went into winter quarters, though he was often in London, and some at least of his forces were also moved to the capital, where there was obviously more accommodation for his men than at Windsor.

Sir William Waller, Essex's colleague, was also at times at Windsor. When Essex was on his western campaign in 1643 Waller was at Windsor with about 2,000 horse and as many foot.

Essex again moved west from Windsor in the summer of 1644, this time advancing far into the south-west, where his forces suffered a disastrous defeat at Lostwithiel in August and Essex himself had to escape by sea. In October, with Waller and Cromwell, he was at Newbury, where the second battle took place on the 27th.

Windsor was the focal point of many of the comings and goings of the Parliamentary armies in 1643 and 1644. In truth, however, the great events of these years were taking place elsewhere, in the West, in the North (where Marston Moor was fought in July 1644) and in East Anglia. But soon, with the formation of the New Model Army, Windsor was once again moving to the centre of the stage.

*Sir William Waller was Parliamentary General, and later a
prisoner at Windsor. (NPG)*

John Hampden. (Margaret Sale)

Rendezvous At Windsor

In the spring of 1645 Windsor saw the mustering of the New Model Army, which was to bring defeat to the King. After almost three years of inconclusive fighting, it was becoming increasingly clear that the war would be won by the side which could organise an efficient army the soonest. By an irony of fate, it was on the parkland and the meadows of what, until 1642, had been *royal* Windsor, that the famous parliamentary army came into being. Day after day saw the arrival of troops and supplies. The new regiments paraded, pike and musket were exercised and manoeuvres were practised. 'Each day', wrote the military historian J.W. Fortescue, 'the scene grew brighter as corps after corps received its new clothing, for the whole army, for the first time in English history, was clad in the familiar scarlet. Facings of the colonels' colours distinguished the regiments and the senior corps of foot, being the general's own, wore his facings of blue. Thus the royal colours, as we now call them, were first seen at the head of a rebel army'.[1]

The earlier campaigns were fought largely by armies of amateurs. On both sides there were officers and men who had seen service on the Continent. In addition those who had served in the armies raised to fight the Scots in 1639 and 1640, or indeed in the local militias and trained bands, must have learned something of drill and discipline. Not even the King, however, had a standing army at his command at the outbreak of war, and Parliament in particular had to improvise an army almost from nothing. Men were found—some volunteered, others were impressed—and the small armies that fought the battles of the Civil War came into being. They learned the perils and the skills of campaigning the hard way, by day to day experience. Early on Cromwell saw the inadequacies of the Parliamentary troops. 'Your troops', he wrote to his cousin Hampden after Edgehill, 'are most of them decayed serving men and tapsters; their troops are gentlemen's sons and persons of quality. Do you think the spirits of such base and mean fellows will ever be able to encounter gentlemen who have courage, resolution and honour in them? You must get men of a spirit that is likely to go as far as gentlemen will go, or you will be beaten still'.

This was the thinking that led to the Eastern Association and eventually to the New Model. At the beginning of 1644 neither side was within sight of final victory. Prince Rupert was the model of the dashing cavalry commander, but much of his activity was dissipated and led to very little. On the Parliamentary side Cromwell still held only a subordinate command and Essex and Manchester, the Parliamentary generals, though by no means incompetent, failed to demonstrate the vigour the situation demanded. Much of the fighting was fragmented, with victories and defeats forming no coherent pattern. Parliament gained strength through its control of most of the ports, of the navy and above all of London. These factors, however, could not by themselves decide the issue of the war.

The Royalists at least possessed a unity of command through the King. Both military and administrative authority were centred in Oxford. Authority on the Parliamentary side was divided between Westminster and Windsor (or wherever the headquarters of the army happened to be). The problem of reconciling the authority of Parliament with the power of the Army existed from the beginning of the war and in fact was never solved, either during the war or after it.

Until his death John Hampden had an especially important role in the co-ordination between Parliament and Army. His frequent journeys between army headquarters at Windsor and the chamber of the House of Commons at Westminster aroused comment even in Oxford. In a lampoon written by the Royalist poet, Sir John Denham, Hampden is made to say:

'Have I so often passed between
Windsor and Westminster, unseen,
    And did myself divide
To keep his Excellence in awe,
And give the Parliament the law?
    For they knew none beside'.[2]

In September 1643 Parliament secured the alliance of the Scots through the Solemn League and Covenant. However, it was not until the following July that the alliance gained its first major success at Marston Moor. The discipline of the Scots was an important factor in the battle, but it was Cromwell and his Ironsides who clinched the victory.

Even so the successes of the Royalist Marquis of Montrose in Scotland and the expectation of help from Ireland kept the King's cause alive. The Parliamentary commanders failed to press home their advantage. 'If we fight a hundred times and beat him ninety-nine times, he will be King still', exclaimed Manchester, 'but if he beat us but once, or the last time, we shall be hanged, we shall lose our estates, and our posterities be undone'. Against this half-heartedness, Cromwell replied bluntly, 'If the army be not put into another method, and the war more vigorously prosecuted, the people can bear the war no longer, and will enforce you to a dishonourable peace'.

The way was paved for the 'new modelling' of the army by the Self-denying Ordinance, by which members of both the House of Commons and the House of Lords gave up their military offices. This meant that

Essex and Manchester—and Cromwell—had to resign, though the way was left open for any of them to be subsequently appointed. The Parliamentary army was to be re-organised on a professional basis. The trained bands and militia would continue to play their part, but it would be a subordinate part. Sir Thomas Fairfax, whose service to the Parliamentary cause had been chiefly in the north of England, was appointed Commander-in-Chief. Philip Skippon, with his background of military experience on the Continent, became Major-General. Cromwell was later appointed second-in-command, but not until 10 June.

The appointment of Fairfax was a decision, the wisdom of which was confirmed by subsequent events. 'He was acceptable to sober men', wrote the Presbyterian divine Richard Baxter, who served for some months as chaplain to a cavalry regiment in the New Model Army, 'because he was religious, faithful, valiant and of a grave sober, resolved disposition'.[3]

He was appointed Captain-General of the New Model Army on 4 February, but did not finally go to Windsor and begin his work there until 3 April. Joshua Sprigge, one of the chaplains of the army, who in his *Anglia Rediviva* wrote a notable contemporary account, said that on 'the 3rd of April he [Fairfax] went from London to Windsor to see, and personally to assist in the framing of the new army; he went in a private manner, purposely avoiding the pomp which usually accompanies a general in the field'.[4] On the last day of the month the New Model Army was ready to march from Windsor. This period of less than four weeks seems incredibly short for the organisation of an army which was to play so momentous a part in the final stages of the war. In point of fact much had been done between the beginning of February and the beginning of April. Fairfax visited Windsor, but for the most part he was in London, choosing and appointing his officers and making arrangements for the mustering of the army. His task was not an easy one. Another contemporary chronicler, John Rushworth, a former assistant clerk to the House of Commons who became Fairfax's secretary, wrote that 'besides fitting the Train for the Field, and the Attendance of the Recruits from London, an entire New Form was to be Introduced into the whole Army, the Forces that remained of the old Army being not only to be Recruited but reduced into New Companies and Regiments, as if they had been newly raised'.[5] Essex's regiments were at Reading and it was feared that the proposed re-organisation might lead to a mutiny. However, Skippon went to Reading on 6 April—it was Easter day—and by his 'prudence and gallantry' won their support.[6] On the same day Fairfax himself was at St Albans, addressing the cavalry.

In the steps leading to the formation of the New Model Army Cromwell's was the initiative and the inspiration. 'Till the whole army were *new modelled*', he said, 'and governed under a stricter discipline, they must not expect any notable success in anything they were about'. Once Fairfax was appointed, Cromwell retired for a time into the background. In the first part of April he was campaigning in Wiltshire, whence he came to Windsor on the 19th to surrender his command in accordance with the Self-denying Ordinance. But the very next day he was directed to take command of a brigade of horse and prevent the King, who was preparing to leave Oxford, from joining with Rupert.

Fairfax's main task at Windsor was to weld the diverse elements of the new army into an efficient fighting force. Sir Samuel Luke, the Parliamentary governor of Newport Pagnell, whose Letter Books are an important source for the Civil War, wrote to Major John Bridges on 11 April: 'From Windsor we hear Sir T Fairfax goes on most successfully and they want not soldiers, they coming to him in such multitudes, and as I hear from Maj Gen Skippon's persuasions all serjeants and corporals which were formerly employed are willing to serve as common soldiers and take both pay, coats and shirts according to the parliamentary allowance. Many other officers listed themselves also. I pray God we find them as ready to march and fight when there is occasion'.[7]

Fairfax was not the commander-in-chief of all the Parliamentary armies. These comprised perhaps 60 or 70,000 in 1645, without counting the Scots. On paper Fairfax was in command of an army of 22,000 men, consisting of 6,600 cavalry, 14,400 infantry and 1,000 dragoons. Many of the infantry had to be raised by impressment, but the cavalry and the dragoons were generally of good quality, especially those that came from Cromwell's Eastern Association. Indeed the contribution of the Eastern Association to the New Model Army was a powerful one; eleven of the New Model's 24 regiments were commanded by Eastern Association officers.

The quality of the officers was in fact the key to the quality of the army. Skippon was the veteran. We are told how he would address the men: 'Come my boys, my brave boys! Let us pray heartily and fight heartily ... Remember the cause is for God, and for the defence of yourselves, your wives and children'.[8]

Many of the officers were young. Fairfax himself was only 33. Col Robert Hammond was 25, Col Ingoldsby 24 and some of the other colonels were almost as young. Among the officers too were many who became leading figures after the War—John Desborough, Henry Ireton, John Okey, Thomas Harrison and Edward Whalley.

The main unifying force of the New Model Army was its moral fervour. It is not necessary to conjure up a vision of an army of saints. It is unlikely that the high standards set by Fairfax were invariably adhered to. Samuel Luke refers at a later time to the drunkenness of some of the infantry (many of whom, unlike the cavalry, were pressed men): 'I think these New Modellers knead all their dough with ale for I never see so many drunk in all my life in so short a time'.[9] But Luke, as several of his letters show, was prejudiced against the New Model and in any case ale, *not* tea, was the common drink of officers and men alike—and there were many inns.

The Army was accompanied by chaplains. To them at least the New Model was going forth on a crusade and the power of their gospel preaching must have brought inspiration to all those whose minds were

*Sir Thomas Fairfax was commander of the New Model
Army. W. Faithorne after R. Walker. (NPG)*

open to receive the word. 'They are an army who understand themselves', wrote John Saltmarsh, one of Fairfax's chaplains; 'God is amongst them'.[10] 'Here men grow religious and more spiritual thriving than in any place of the kingdom' declared Hugh Peters, the most famous of the army's preachers.[11]

Fairfax issued a Code of Conduct, known as the *Articles of War*. The first section treated of 'duties to God'. Blasphemy was to be punished by having the 'tongue bored with a red-hot iron', cursing by loss of pay, and neglect to attend divine worship by 'severe censure'. Of offences against 'moral duties', drunkenness would be subject to the jurisdiction of a court martial, while crimes such as 'rapes, ravishments and unnatural abuses' were punishable by death. Theft, pillage and murder were also, in extreme cases, to meet with the death penalty. There were strict regulations about the behaviour of the troops on the move: 'no soldier shall presume, in marching or lodging, to cut down any fruit trees, or to deface or spoil walks of trees, upon pain of severe punishment'.[12] From the beginning Fairfax tried to ensure that all men received 'coat and conduct money, wages and entertainments, and other necessary charges and allowances'.[13]

How was the New Model Army accommodated during its four weeks at Windsor? It could not have been accommodated in the town alone. Apart from the continuing presence of the Castle garrison, the New Model Army amounted to more than ten times the population of Windsor. Tents seem the obvious answer. C.H. Firth, however, in his standard book on *Cromwell's Army* says: 'During the earlier part of the Civil War tents were not used by either side. The soldiers of the New Model Army during the campaign of 1645 either bivouacked in the open air or were quartered in villages. In the English army of the period tents were first introduced when it served outside England, in less populous countries such as Ireland and Scotland'.[14] So the probability is that, as had been the case with the armies of Essex and Waller when they were based on Windsor, the New Model Army was quartered in the towns and villages of the neighbourhood. Whatever the truth of this, these must have been exciting days for the people of Windsor as well as for the Eton boys across the river.

The despatch of supplies for the New Model Army continued up to the last moment. On 29 April the Commons ordered that 1,000 saddles, bridles and furniture, 1,000 pair of pistols and holsters, and 500 pair of spare holsters should be sent to Windsor 'for this present expedition'. The urgency was underlined by the further order: 'That five of the Members of the House which are of the Committee of the Army do presently withdraw and sign warrants for sending away the Saddles, Pistols and other Provisions ordered to be sent to Windsor, and for the issuing of Fifteen Thousand Pounds to be sent to the Army'.[15]

Even after the departure of the New Model Army, Windsor continued to serve as a base for Fairfax. Another Deputy Muster Master was sent to Windsor at the beginning of May 'to muster the recruits that are coming up'. Pressed men were still being sent to Windsor at the end of the month 'that they should be sent to the army'. Money for the use of the Army was also sent to Windsor and Fairfax was told to 'send a convoy to be there at that time'.[16]

The New Model Army left Windsor on 30 April and marched to Reading. Its immediate purpose was to relieve Taunton, where Col Blake, short of both food and fodder, still defied the King's Army. Samuel Luke, however, says that (of the 22,000) '9,000 were appointed for the West and 13,000 under Lt Gen Cromwell and Maj General Browne to secure Oxford'. He also says that Fairfax himself was 'left sick at Windsor'. Sprigge more explicitly says that the General was 'under an indisposition of body, by reason of an ague that had exercised him for some time'. Be that as it may, Fairfax was certainly with his troops a day or two later.[17]

From Reading Fairfax marched by way of Theale to Newbury, whither he summoned Cromwell—then engaged in an attack on Faringdon, one of the few places in Berkshire still in Royalist hands—for consultation. A confused period follows. The mere threat of the approach of the Parliamentary army led the Royalists to raise the siege of Taunton. When, however, Fairfax turned back to besiege Oxford he found that the King had left and, with Rupert, was active in the Midlands in a campaign that led to the storming of Leicester at the end of May. Fairfax stayed for some days in the neighbourhood of Oxford, but then marched north to counter the King's movements.

On 12 June Cromwell, now officially appointed as Lieutenant-General of Horse, joined Fairfax near Northampton. Two days later the battle of Naseby took place between Rugby and Kettering and the New Model Army won its first decisive victory. The Royalist army was shattered, and nearly 5,000 prisoners, all the King's artillery and baggage and his incriminating private papers fell into the hands of the victors. The New Model then turned upon the hitherto victorious Royalist army of the south-west and in July, at the battle of Langport, near Bridgwater, routed that army too.

The Royalists fought a series of desperate rearguard actions that prolonged their resistance into the next year. But with the capture of Oxford in June 1646 the war came to a virtual end and Parliament, or rather the Parliamentary army, had triumphed. 'You have done your work',said Royalist Jacob Astley after his capture at Stow-on-the-Wold in March,'*and may go play, unless you fall out among yourselves*'.[18]

Charles, disguised as a serving-man, escaped from Oxford on 27 April in the company of Michael Hudson, the chaplain, and John Ashburnham, a Groom of the Bedchamber. Making his way in the direction of London, he may have been near enough to Windsor to see the Castle on its hill to the south. Certainly from the ridge from Hillingdon to Harrow he could look out over London. However, any idea of entering the capital was abandoned, and turning north, he put himself in the hands of the Scots.

Oliver Cromwell. Miniature by S. Cooper. (NPG)

Untrodden Paths

The surrender of the King and the fall of Oxford brought military victory to the Parliamentary cause, but they did not bring a solution to the problems that had caused the war. Another two and a half years passed before the execution of the King opened up the way to revolutionary solutions such as had seemed wholly undesirable to most men in 1646. They were years full of uncertainty, frustration and strife.

The King had surrendered to the Scots. It was, he hoped, a move based on shrewd calculations. Ancestral associations would count for something surely, for the Stuarts were the Scottish Royal Family and Charles himself was King of Scotland. The Scots had entered the war on the side of Parliament in order to secure and advance the cause of presbyterianism, and Charles thought he could play upon the distrust which had arisen between the Scots and Parliament.

In the short term he failed. The Scots held the King at Newcastle from May 1646 to January 1647, but then surrendered him to Parliament. In the long term, however, his hopes were rewarded when the Scots supported the Royalist cause in the Second Civil War in 1648. Their support revived after the King's execution and it required the Parliamentary victories of Dunbar in 1650 and Worcester in 1651 before the Scots were forced into peace.

The Civil War had been won by the Army and after its military victory it became increasingly conscious of its power. The interminable postponements of pay caused deep discontent. It was, however, the differences over 'the settlement of the nation', both political and religious , that drove a wedge between Army and Parliament.

The Army had developed a strong *esprit de corps*. It had accepted a wide diversity of religious opinions in its ranks during the war. Joshua Sprigge had written, 'They prospered more in their unity than in their uniformity'. The Independents, as they came to be called, believed in a wide-ranging toleration in peace. Many of the Army's leaders, including Cromwell himself, were Independents. The Army was resolved not to submit to the imposition of the rigid presbyterian system to which Parliament was pledged. 'New presbyter is but old priest writ large', wrote John Milton.

Their political views were even more radical. They developed a quasi-political organisation within the Army, with Agitators—two for each regiment—to represent their grievances. The more extreme, the left-wing as we should say to-day, bore the name of Levellers. Their chief leader and spokesman was the fiery radical thinker, John Lilburne. They argued, they agitated, they drafted manifestoes like *The Agreement of the People,* demanding biennial parliaments, equal constituencies and manhood suffrage.

Parliament, not surprisingly, was anxious to get rid of so formidable a rival. Since the war was over, the Army could be disbanded or sent to Ireland to deal with the rebels there. The Army, however, refused to disband or to keep quiet in the controversies of the time. In 1647 the Army seized the King at Holmby House in Northamptonshire, where Parliament had been holding him, and kept him in their own charge.

So the King passed from the control of the Scots into the hands of Parliament and thence into the less tolerant control of the Army. Isolated from his friends, Charles still maintained his faith that his restoration to power was only a matter of time. He carried on a series of intrigues, often skilful, whose chief effect was to convince each party in turn that he was untrustworthy. Cromwell expressed his view of the King in the House of Commons in January 1648. 'The King', he declared. 'was a man of great parts and a great understanding, but ... so great a dissembler and so false a man that he was not to be trusted'. Charles was prepared to receive proposals, to take his time in composing answers, while he had no serious intention of arriving at a lasting settlement based on surrendering any of the powers which he considered to be his by divine right.

When the New Model Army left Windsor at the end of April 1645, the Castle garrison remained. In June Colonel Christopher Whichcot, who had been Sergeant Major General of the London Brigade under Essex, took the place of John Venn as Governor. The Corporation paid their respects both to the outgoing and to the incoming Governor. The chamberlain's accounts note that on 26 June a sum of 19s was paid 'for a gallon of brewed wine and 4 loaves of Sugar weighing xi lbs at 16d per lb when Mr Mayor and some of his Company went to Colonel Venn at his going away from the Castle'. And ten days later, on 6 July, £1 7s 3d was paid 'for wine and 4 loaves of sugar weighing xii lbs at 16d per lb, and 3s 6d given to the Court of Guard and sentinel, when Mr Mayor, Mr Day, Mr Starkey, Mr Trew and 8 more of their Company went to visit Colonel Whichcot, with a quart of Sack Mr Mayor gave him when he first came to this Town'.

Whichcot was plunged straight away into the problem of providing for the garrison under his charge. There was trouble immediately on his arrival and it is interesting to note that it was again the Common Council of London which urged the Commons to make adequate provision for Windsor. They referred to 'the sense the City has of the importance of that place, and of the condition it is now in; and their earnest desire that particular and present care may be taken of it'. As an immediate step the

House resolved that £400 should be advanced for the supply and subsistence of the garrison and a Committee (including John Venn and Cornelius Holland) was appointed 'to consider of an establishment for the garrison of Windsor, and how out of the neighbouring towns and hundreds or otherwise this Garrison may be maintained'.[1]

In March 1646 the officers and soldiers of the Windsor garrison petitioned the Lords, stating that they were in great want of pay, being 90 weeks behind. This petition was followed by discussions about the sale of a brass statue at the Castle and a Garter Collar. There was also discussion of 'five and twenty hundred pounds informed to be hidden under-ground in some private place in or about Windsor Castle'. The Garter Collar was that presented to Gustavus Adolphus, King of Sweden, when he became a Knight of the Order. It was said to excel 'for richness and glory' all others bestowed by former sovereigns, each letter of the motto *Honi soit qui mal y pense* being composed of diamonds. It was returned to Windsor after his death in 1632. When the War broke out it had been hidden, as we have seen, under the floor of the Treasury Chamber adjoining St George's Chapel. It was Cornelius Holland who ferreted out the secret of its hiding place and in March 1645 the Garter was delivered to Col Venn and subsequently to Col Whichcot, who handed it to John Hunt, treasurer to the trustees appointed by the Parliament for the sale of the King's goods, and sold by him to Thomas Beauchamp, their clerk.[2]

These frantic attempts to produce money for the payment of the garrison must have met with some success, because when we next hear about arrears of pay in July 1647 it was now a mere 'twelvemonth'. In that month Fairfax wrote to the Speaker of the Commons from Aylesbury: 'Understanding the small force is left in Windsor Castle, and considering the consequence of that place, which I thought it my duty to acquaint you withal; and further, to desire you that you will please to move the house for some pay for that garrison, which, as I understand, is about a twelvemonth in arrear, and since March last hath not received one penny'.[3]

Few months passed without complaints and requests for more money. In November 1647, when the Army headquarters were again at Windsor, disbanded soldiers flocked thither demanding either money to carry them to their homes or else to be re-admitted to their regiments. The officers at Windsor were willing to pay them money to carry them home; but unfortunately the second instalment of the month's pay of the army did not reach Windsor for some days after it was due, and consequently most of the soldiers were in the meantime sent back to their regiments.[4]

Money was constantly needed, not only for the payment of the garrison, but also to discharge the obligations incurred under the system of quartering troops on the local inhabitants. The abuse of this practice aroused bitter complaints. Some of the local grievances are expressed in a petition to the Commons on 9 December from 'divers Freeholders,

Farmers and Labourers in that part of the county of Bucks which is near adjoining to Windsor Castle, complaining both of free quarter and the withholding of the army's pay'.[5]

The outbreak of the Second Civil War in May 1648 made matters even more urgent. Fairfax wrote from Windsor to the Committee of the Army on 26 May urging a supply of money for the Castle. He says: 'I cannot but mind your lordships again, of the great necessity of some present assignment of moneys for the better fortifying and victualling of this castle'.[6] This letter had some effect, for on its being reported to the House of Commons the House ordered on the following day that £1,500 should be paid to Col Whichcot 'to be employed for furnishing it with Victuals, and making the necessary Fortifications of that Castle'. The House ordered further 'that the Committee of the Army do take care to furnish the Garrison of Windsor Castle with a hundred beds, of those that were provided for the Soldiers in the Tower of London'.[7]

This was at the end of May. In July Whichcot was still complaining that the Castle was 'full of want and full of danger' and adding that he feared more from the soldiers of the garrison than from the enemy outside.[8]

As far as we can tell, Windsor town remained true to its puritan allegiance and there is much evidence of the close association which existed between town and Castle.

The Puritans were able to take full control of the religious life of the town. They did not create separate non-conforming churches; they took over the Church and re-modelled it along puritan lines. By the Solemn League and Covenant with the Scots, accepted by the Commons in Sepetember 1643, the office of bishop had been abolished and in January 1645 the use of the Book of Common Prayer was made illegal. Alongside these fundamental changes went many others to bring the practices of the Church into harmony with puritan principles. Altar rails were removed; the communion table was shifted into the centre of the church; in many churches stained glass and images were destroyed or defaced; the practice of bowing to the altar ceased; surplices were discarded; the sermon was exalted to the place of prime importance; many of the clergy who would not conform were dispossessed.

The Vicar of Windsor since 1633 had been the Laudian John Cleaver. His authority was certainly qualified during the Civil War period, but he does not seem to have been completely ousted. His name, for example, does not appear after 1640 as one of those by whom the churchwardens' accounts were allowed and passed, but money paid to the poor in 1642-3 is stated to be paid 'with consent of John Cleaver vicar'. Only a little while before his death in 1648 he was still signing 'Joh'es Cleaver vicarius'. The entry for his burial reads: 'October 22. Mr John Cleaver, our worthy minister'.

Other ministers also occupied the pulpit of the Parish Church. The practice approximated to that of a present-day Free Church, where the pulpit is shared week by week by the resident minister, visiting ministers and lay preachers. Again, as with the matters concerned with the maintenance of the Garrison in the Castle, the House of Commons seems to have found time, among its multifarious responsibilities, to provide for the needs of the Windsor Parish Church.

On 1 December 1646 the Committee of the House of Commons for Plundered Ministers ordered that the yearly sum of £50 should be paid out of the rents and possessions of the 'Dean and Chapter of Windsor, in New Windsor, in the County of Berks', 'to and for increase of the maintenance of such ministers as should officiate in the parish Church of New Windsor'. The same Committee, on 23 January 1647, ordered that the £50 should be paid 'during the Incumbancy of Mr Cleaver the present vicar of the said Parish Church to such Minister as this Committee shall appoint from time to time, to officiate in the said parish Church; and not unto the said Vicar. And this Committee do for the present authorise and appoint the Mayor of the said Town and Col Whichcot Governor of the Castle of Windsor to receive the said maintenance of £50 a year, for three months next ensuing, and all arrears thereof, and pay the same to such person or persons as they shall appoint to officiate in the said Church during the said time'.

Six persons were appointed 'to nominate him that shall perform or officiate the Lecture in the parish Church'. They included the Mayor, Col Whichcot and Matthew Day, Windsor's veteran citizen—he had been Mayor as far back as 1610. Twelve individuals were nominated by them. These included Sir Robert Bennett, who had twice represented Windsor in Parliament in the 1620s, and Mr George Starkey, a former Mayor. The list also included 'Mr Brown the Butcher', but who is to say that a butcher cannot also be an acceptable preacher? In any event he rose to the position of Mayor in 1657.

Later, in April 1648, an ordinance was passed in the House of Lords 'for appointing three Ministers to preach at Windsor, and to have £100 yearly apiece for their maintenance'.[9]

St George's Chapel was also witness to the current changes. The ejection of the Dean and Canons in 1643 paved the way for the transformation of the Chapel into a puritan place of worship. As with the Parish Church, we know the names of some of the ministers who officiated in the Chapel. There was, for example, a prominent Independent minister named John Bachelor. In 1643 he had been appointed as one of the licensers for printing books of divinity and his activity in that office led to presbyterian complaints of his sanctioning all sorts of sectarian literature, including that of advocates of toleration. He was made a Fellow of Eton in 1647 and later became Vice-Provost. Closely associated with him, both at St George's and at Eton, was Nicholas Lockyer. At St George's he gained a reputation as a fervent and powerful preacher. He was one of Cromwell's chaplains and became Provost of Eton in 1659. His tenure of that coveted office lasted only a year, for he was ejected at the Restoration and for a period lived in exile in Holland. No doubt, when the Army was at Windsor, some of the leading Puritan chaplains such as Hugh Peters, Edward Bowles and John Saltmarsh occupied the pulpit.

One of Windsor's leading Independents throughout the 1640s was Cornelius Holland, Windsor's radical MP. He emerges from the story of these years as a typically militant puritan. He does not seem to have taken a prominent part in the debates of the Long Parliament before the War, but the importance of Windsor during the War obviously increased his own importance. It was at this time perhaps that he first began to act as a link-man between Parliament and Army—a role he was well qualified to fulfil as a Windsor MP. He never, as was the case with many MPs from Cromwell downwards, sought to be a soldier. He was therefore all the more able to devote his time to his Parliamentary duties. Once the war started Parliament had to assume executive as well as legislative functions and Cornelius Holland was assiduous in his service to the parliamentary cause. He served, for example, on the 'Committee for sick and maimed soldiers, for regulation of the patients and nurses in the Savoy and other hospitals'.[10] This was obviously one of his special spheres of interest and he played a leading part in securing provision in the Castle for 'such Soldiers as have been maimed in the Parliament's service; and for such Widows, fatherless Children, and Orphans, whose Husbands and Fathers have been slain in the Parliament's Service'.[11]

He supported the steps which led to the formation of the New Model Army and as early as March 1644 he was one of the members of a Commons Committee—'all violent spirits' as one of Holland's Parliamentary colleagues described them—named to investigate the officers in Essex's army and make a list of those who should be removed. In the following month he was prominent in opposing the attempt to establish a presbyterian system in the country in the wake of the Solemn League and Covenant.[12] At Westminster he must have spent much of his time serving on committees—his name occurs frequently in the Commons Journals. But he was also often at Windsor, concerning himself with soldiers' pay, disorders in the Park, buried treasure in the Castle, the ordering of the religious life of the town, co-ordination between Town and Castle . . .

What may be the only surviving letter from him we owe to the zeal of Sir Samuel Luke in preserving his correspondence in his *Letter Books*. In March 1645 Holland was trying to persuade Luke, as Governor of Newport Pagnell, to do a favour to a young protegé who was obviously a sectary with extremist views. Luke, a Presbyterian, was trying to free the town of sectaries, accusing them of practising free love and the destruction of 'Magistracy or government'. So he was unwilling to accede to Holland's insistence and felt so strongly that he wrote to Holland: 'I am sorry your eyes should be so blinded, and your judgment so darkened, as to believe a man who is refractory, both to the ecclesiastical, civil and martial discipline now practised, should be fit to live in a garrison town'. Holland's comment on his disagreement with Luke was: 'Let not us who are all for heaven part in our way thither upon differences in opinions upon things that, if well considered, will no ways hinder us to our journey's end, but let love cover the multitude of all our infirmities and failings'. The furthest Luke was prepared to go was to offer to defer to the judgment of the House of Commons: 'if you let the House be acquainted with this, if they command his stay, their commands shall be obeyed'.[13]

Following the end of the War, Holland was one of the parliamentary commissioners appointed to negotiate the treaty with the Scots. The end of the War in fact increased his importance, although it is often difficult to find out where he was and what he was doing at any particular time. Important as he may have become, more especially perhaps in his own estimation, he was not important enough for his career to be documented in such a way as, say, Cromwell's. In any case Holland was a civilian and during the years from 1646 to 1648 the soldiers were increasingly in the driving seats. One thing is clear, however; he was not at any time a member of the peace party who wanted reconciliation with the King at almost any price.

After an interval of more than five years, the King visited Windsor in July 1647, but in different circumstances than when he came there with the Queen at the beginning of 1642. Even then he had been virtually a fugitive from his capital but he was still master of his own movements. Now, although he was still treated outwardly with the respect due to his rank, he was in all essentials a prisoner.

After Charles had been forcibly removed from Holmby House, he was moved from place to place according to the movements of the army 'being in all places', as Clarendon said, 'as well provided for and accommodated as he had used to be in any progress; the best gentlemen of the several counties through which he passed daily resorted to him without distinction; he was attended by some of his old trusty servants in the places nearest his person'.[14]

It is said that Charles himself expressed a wish to go to Windsor and he arrived at the Castle from Hatfield on 1 July. The bells of the Parish Church were rung at his coming. He hoped to meet his children, the Duke of York, the Duke of Gloucester and Princess Elizabeth, who at this time were under the care of the Earl of Northumberland at Syon House at Brentford. His expectations were, however, disappointed, although he was given the opportunity of seeing them two weeks later at Maidenhead. Col Whichcot was ordered to remove Dr Sheldon and Dr Hammond, Charles' chaplains, as well as others, but they seem to have been restored to the King when he left Windsor on the 3rd to stay with Lord Craven at Caversham near Reading.

After the Civil War ended in 1646 the headquarters of the Army moved around considerably—London, Newmarket, Saffron Walden, St Albans, Bury St Edmunds, Reading, Putney, Windsor.

In October 1647 they were at Putney and it was there that some of the most famous of the political debates among the army officers took place. On 28 October 'The Agreement of the People for a firm and present peace upon grounds of common right' was presented to the General Council of the Army.

The General Council had evolved from the councils of war which became customary during the later stages of the Civil War. By 1647 it had become the organ through which the opinion of the Army found expression.

At the beginning of November the Army Headquarters were moved to Windsor, where they remained until the outbreak of the Second Civil War in May 1648. These six months witnessed the holding at Windsor of a series of meetings of the General Council which played a vital part in the course of events. Not long after his brief sojourn at Windsor, the King had been taken to Hampton Court. He was obviously well-informed about what was happening in Army circles and believed there might be an attempt to assassinate him. On the night of 15 November he made a dramatic escape and, although he was subsequently captured and imprisoned in Carisbrooke Castle in the Isle of Wight, this further evidence of the King's untrustworthiness opened a little wider the door which was to lead just over a year later to his trial and execution. Sir John Berkeley brought letters from the King to the generals at Windsor on 28 November. He related how Cromwell, Ireton and others who were present 'saluted me very coldly and had their countenances quite changed towards me'.[15]

Three days before Sir John's visit there had been a meeting of the General Council, not in the Castle, but at the Town Hall at Windsor. It dealt mainly with questions of army pay and the problems of free quarter, rather than with fundamental political issues, and could well have taken the form of a conference with representatives of the various bodies (including the Corporation of Windsor), which had to serve the Army's needs.[16]

Many of the meetings of the Army General Council were accompanied by prayer meetings. The officers were only too well aware that they were following untrodden paths and needed to wait upon the Lord to know His will before they acted. It is easy perhaps to mock at the prayers and preachings of these puritan leaders, but they moved in a world where things of the spirit were real and, in face of the duplicity of the King, the antagonism of Parliament and the rising tides of ill-will around them, they sought the guidance that would lead them in the way of truth.

An example is the meeting at the Castle on 21 and 22 December 1647. On the first day the officers dealt with disciplinary questions and 'the present juncture of affairs'. The following day, as John Rushworth tells us, 'was according to appointment kept as a general fast by the General and officers; the duties of the day were performed by divers of the officers, amongst whom there was a sweet harmony, the Lieutenant-General [Cromwell], Commissary-General Ireton, Col Tichborne, Col Hewson, Mr Peters and other officers prayed very fervently and pathetically; this continued from nine in the morning till seven at night'.[17]

There were further meetings on the 28th to the 30th, when the Commissioners of the Parliament were present. The Commissioners and the Officers joined in prayer 'and other things tending to the good of the Kingdom and Army'. On the 30th, Cromwell, Ireton and other chief officers dined with the Commissioners 'and with much love parted from them when they took their leave for London, and the Castle gave them a salute with Five and Twenty Pieces of Ordnance'.[18]

Already there were rumours that Charles had concluded a secret agreement to bring in the Scots. Throughout the first four months of 1648 the Army Officers were putting their forces in a state of readiness. Meeting followed meeting until at the end of April the General Council met at Windsor in what was perhaps the most crucial conclave of all.

One of those present was Adjutant-General Allen and years afterwards, in 1659, when the puritan world was falling to pieces, he described this dramatic three-day meeting in *A faithful Memorial of that remarkable meeting of many Officers of the Army in England at Windsor Castle, in the year 1648*.[19]

To the Puritans every success was a sign of Divine favour and every failure a sign of Divine wrath. So, as they faced the imminent prospect of a renewal of the war, the Officers spent many hours in heart-searching praying and preaching. By the third day, Monday, 1 May, they had reached their conclusion; they had sinned against the Lord in trying to reach a settlement with the King. 'We were led', said Allen in his narrative, 'to a clear understanding among ourselves, not any dissenting, that it was the duty of our day, with the forces we had, to go out and fight against those potent enemies, which that year in all places appeared against us, with a humble confidence, in the name of the Lord only, that we should destroy them. And we were also enabled then, after serious seeking His face, to come to a very clear and joint resolution . . . that it was our duty, if ever the Lord brought us back again in peace, to call Charles Stuart, that man of blood, to an account for that blood he had shed, and mischief he had done to his utmost, against the Lord's Cause and People in these poor Nations'.

While the Officers were meeting, the news was confirmed that South Wales was in a state of revolt. As they braced themselves to face the challenge, they knew that their enemies would rise on every side. Action must follow prayer. On 3 May Cromwell set out westwards from Windsor with two regiments of horse and three of foot. The Second Civil War had begun.

Henry Ireton, Parliamentary general; son-in-law of Cromwell. Prominent in Windsor, especially in 1648 Attributed to R. Walker. (NPG)

This Great Business

The Second Civil War in 1648 sealed the fate of the King. Like the First, the Second Civil War was a fragmented war, but it still represented a threat to the victory won in 1646. With co-ordination it could indeed have been successful in its objective of restoring the King; but with Charles a prisoner in the hands of the Army it lacked a unified command.

South Wales was the first to rise in revolt. Most of Kent and Essex rose for the King in the second half of May. The fleet mutinied. The Scots, however, on whom rested the chief hopes of success, did not cross the border until 8 July and by this time Fairfax had suppressed the rising in Kent and was besieging Colchester. Pembroke capitulated to Cromwell on 11 July so that he was left free to march north to meet the Scots. The final blow was delayed, while the opposing armies manoeuvred for position. In mid-August Cromwell defeated the Scots in a three-day running battle in Lancashire. On the 28th Colchester surrendered and the Second Civil War was virtually over.

The risings had been suppressed, but through the summer no one could prophesy from which quarter the next danger would come. In June fears had been entertained of a Royalist attempt to seize Windsor Castle. There were rumours that the Royalists would use the midsummer fair as a cover for concentrating in the town as a preliminary to action. Message after message was despatched by 'the Committee of both Houses', which was in charge. One of the most graphic of these is that sent on the 22nd to the Buckinghamshire Committee. 'We are informed', it begins, 'there is now some design upon the castle of Windsor; you know the consequence of that place to the kingdom, and the danger it would bring to your county among others if it should be surprised by the enemy. There being a fair to be held at Windsor on Saturday next, it may prove dangerous owing to the concourse of many thither under that pretence. We have received a desire from the Governor for some horse to be sent thither, but all those of the Army are so employed as none can be spared at present. We are informed that through your good affection to the public and seasonal regard to your own safety there is a troop now ready in your county under Major Shalford, which you should cause to march towards Windsor and quarter thereabout, as may be best for the defence and safety of that castle. In regard of the occasion of the fair do not fail to have your troop there to-morrow at night, and upon your march advertise the Governor of the Castle of your coming'.[1] The alarm persisted into July, but by August the same Committee was writing to Whichcot about a threat to Winchester and ordering him to 'send what horse you conveniently can to those places on the road, to seize those persons and horses lying there whereby their designs may be frustrated'.[2]

Another notable influx of Royalist prisoners followed the Second Civil War. This time, however, the prisoners in many cases were treated not as honourable opponents but as rebels. The suppression of the rising in South Wales brought Col Poyer, Major-General Richard Laugharne (both defectors from the Parliamentary cause) and Col R. Powell to Windsor. All three were condemned to death; but as an act of clemency they were allowed to draw lots to determine which one of the three should go to the block. It was Poyer.

The leader of the Kent rising, Sir Thomas Peyton was confined in the Castle. Sixteen well-to-do London citizens, suspected of being implicated in a Royalist plot, were seized in their beds and brought to Windsor. After Cromwell's defeat of the Scots at Preston, their Royalist commander, the Duke of Hamilton, a cousin of the King, was lodged in the Castle until his escape at the end of January 1649.

The severest treatment was reserved for the Royalists taken after the siege of Colchester by Fairfax. Earlier calls for surrender had been ignored and no mercy was shown after the town was eventually taken. The common soldiers (amounting to between three and four thousand) were sent to Bristol and other sea towns, previous to transportation to America, Venice and other places, where they were sold as slaves. Some of the Lords 'with two men apiece, and twelve other officers' were brought to Windsor. Lord Goring, Lord Capel and Lord Loughborough were among them. Capel was executed; Goring was saved from the same fate by the Speaker's casting vote; Loughborough escaped.

There was even a notorious sea captain in the Castle at this time. This was Captain Browne Bushell who, being put in command of a fine new Parliamentary ship, handed it over to the Royalists. For this he spent three years in Windsor Castle, where he used some of his time following the fashion of carving his name and coat of arms. Eventually, Parliament resolved that 'Captain Browne Bushell, the great Sea Agent against the Parliament' should be exempted from mercy, and he was executed in 1651.

In the meantime Charles was still at Carisbrooke. The defection of the fleet raised doubts as to whether or not it was advisable to leave him in the Isle of Wight, but proposals (made as early as 23 June) to move him to Windsor were unsuccessful. Discussions about his future became, however, increasingly urgent and in the temper of the Army after the Second Civil War moderate counsels fought a losing battle.

Parliament was nonetheless still hoping for a settlement with the King. Negotiations had dragged on from the end of the First Civil War, through the remainder of 1646, and throughout the whole of 1647, until in January 1648, Parliament in disillusionment passed the 'Vote of No Addresses', breaking off further communications. Later in the year, however, despite the Second Civil War, Parliament made further overtures to Charles, and Commissioners were sent to Newport in the Isle of Wight to re-open discussions with him. From these discussions came the so-called Treaty of Newport.

As late as 15 November the House voted for the King's restoration, if the Newport proposals were accepted. Some of the Army leaders themselves, especially Fairfax, were against extreme measures. Cromwell was still sitting on the fence. Others, such as Ireton, had no doubt that the time had come to execute justice on the King.

The headquarters of the Army, which for some time had been at St Albans, were again transferred to Windsor on 24 November 1648 and, from this time, until the King was finally taken to London in the following January to face his trial, Windsor was once again at the centre of events. The very next day the Council of Officers 'held long debate' in the Castle and from this point events moved fast.

It seems that Ireton had been at Windsor for some time, drawing up a Remonstrance from the Army to Parliament, demanding the trial of the King. Married to Cromwell's daughter, Bridget, Ireton was probably the ablest politian in the Army; his premature death in Ireland in 1651 deprived the Commonwealth of one of its most capable and committed leaders. By early November the Remonstrance, with its demands for a purge of Parliament and the trial of the King, was before Fairfax and his Council of Officers, with Ireton urging immediate action. On the 20th the Remonstrance was presented to the Commons. Cornelius Holland was one of the members who welcomed it, but otherwise it was brushed aside.

Ireton now turned his attention to a new draft of *The Agreement of the People,* which sought to provide a framework for a new political order for the country. Ireton may have had a talent for drawing up constitutions, but the Levellers had all the distrust of revolutionaries for the merely radical reformer and it seems that, while the Army headquarters were still at St Albans, they heard of the Remonstrance and judged that it was 'requisite for some of us to go to Windsor to speak with Ireton—the steersman himself'.

Further meetings were certainly held after the Army headquarters had moved to Windsor. Lilburne and his Leveller colleagues stayed at the Garter Inn immortalised by Shakespeare in *The Merry Wives of Windsor.* It is depicted in Norden's *View* next to the White Hart and almost opposite the Castle Hill. It is shown as having a massive porch, with a courtyard in the rear. It was destroyed by fire in 1681.

Ireton came down from the Castle to meet the Levellers. He was 'accompanied by a whole train of officers' and 'a large and sharp discourse ensued'. The Levellers secured Ireton's concurrence in their proposal for a Committee of 16, representing the Army, Parliament, Independents and Levellers, to be formed to draw up the Agreement.

Cornelius Holland did not of course participate in the crucial Army meetings at the Castle, but he was in Windsor on 26 November and probably the following days when he took part in the talks at the Garter. Lilburne and his friends returned to London to meet and choose representatives. They then came back to Windsor and held a meeting in the 'Council Chamber' at the Castle. Little progress was made, for the Army leaders at this moment had other things on their mind.[3]

On 30 November Colonel Ewer was sent from Windsor to take the King from the Isle of Wight to Hurst Castle, a bleak fortress on the mainland shore of the Solent. Here he was held while the plans for bringing him to trial were worked out. The Army leaders at Windsor prayed and consulted. More and more petitions arrived from regiments stationed in South Wales and the North, demanding justice on the King. Fairfax wrote to Cromwell, who was still with the Army in the north, requiring his attendance 'with all convenient speed' so as to give 'a merciful furtherance . . . to this very great business now in agitation'.[4]

Parliament in the meantime was still pursuing its policy of exploring ways and means of restoring the King. During the first five days of December, a protracted debate led to a decision to accept the Newport proposals as a basis for further negotiations. By the time the decision was reached, however, the Army had marched from Windsor to London and was in complete control. On the morning of the 6th, a party of troops under Col Pride stood at the door of the House of Commons and excluded 96 members and arrested 45 more. Others thought that discretion was the better part of valour and kept away. Cornelius Holland was again prominent. He may have been a member of the small committee, consisting of three officers and three civilian MPs, who made the arrangements for the Purge. They agreed that only members 'faithful to the public interest' should be allowed to enter the House. 'To this end', says Holland's republican colleague Edmund Ludlow, 'we went over the names of all the members one by one, giving the truest characters we could of their inclinations'.[5] When the Purge took place, Richard Winwood, Holland's fellow MP for Windsor, was one of those excluded. Cromwell returned to London on the following day. He said that 'he had not been acquainted with this design; yet, since it was done, he was glad of it'.

On 15 December the Council of Officers decided that the King should be brought to Windsor 'in order to the bringing of him speedily to justice'. Thomas Herbert, the King's personal attendant, writing many years afterwards, said that 'So soon as the King heard Windsor named, he seemed to rejoice in it . . . Windsor was a place he ever delighted in'.[6] Perhaps the very mention of Windsor aroused memories of happier days. Now his family was scattered; courtiers who might have brought him some companionship and attention were debarred from his presence. Only his two dogs—the greyhound Gypsy and the spaniel Rogue—remained to befriend him. They accompanied him from Hurst

Castle to Windsor and were with him during the time of his trial in London until, at some point during the closing days, they were removed at his own request. At all times the King's strong religious faith sustained him as the final tragedy drew nearer.

The King left Hurst Castle under strong guard on Tuesday the 19th. He made no use of his coach and rode on horseback. When he reached Winchester, the Mayor and Aldermen were ready to receive him with traditional ceremony. The mace was handed to him and formally returned and, as he entered the city, many of the gentry and citizens pressed forward to pay their respects. The Mayor was afterwards reprimanded, but at the time there seems to have been no attempt to prevent these manifestations of loyalty.

It was, however, the last such occasion. Before he reached Farnham at the end of the second day of his journey, he had come under the escort of Col Thomas Harrison, with a large body of horsemen. Harrison had the reputation of being a fanatical puritan. He it was who had first pointed the finger at 'Charles Stuart, that man of blood' and a few weeks later he was to be one of those who signed the King's death-warrant. And yet, improbably, his appearance belied his reputation. 'Fine and gilded' were epithets applied to him by John Lilburne and, when he joined the King as he approached Farnham from Alton, observers noted that Harrison had a velvet hat on his head and wore a new buffcoat, with a 'crimson silk scarf about his waist, richly fringed'. He maintained at least an outward courtesy towards the King.

From Farnham to Windsor was a journey of some 25 miles across the heaths and forest lands of Surrey and Berkshire. The day was wet and cold and the roads muddy. The party stopped at Bagshot, near the half-way point, and the King dined with Lord and Lady Newburgh. The King's horse had gone lame; 'a piece of a Nail had unfortunately run into his Foot, at which His Majesty was much troubled'. His host, a racing man and a Royalist, was ready to provide a fast horse, 'a brave Gelding, which the Party was somewhat fearful might be too light of foot for them'. Harrison, however, was far too vigilant. The King was placed in the middle of a hundred horse, every soldier having a pistol 'ready spanned' in his hand and the journey continued through driving rain and the gathering darkness of the brief December afternoon.

There was no Mayoral welcome in Windsor and the bells of the Parish Church, which had been rung even at the King's last coming to Windsor in the previous year, remained silent. Many townspeople, however, resorted to the 'town's-end' and 'upon his Majesty passing by, a great echo arose from the voice of the people, crying "God bless your majesty, and send you long to reign" '.

Some of these descriptive details of the King's sad homecoming come from a pamphlet entitled *Terrible and Bloody News from Windsor*. It goes on to narrate how, after the King had finally reached the Castle, some of the Royalists had resorted to the inns of the town and begun to drink to the King's health. Musketeers from the Castle Guard were sent to deal with them. The Royalists resisted and three men were killed and several wounded before the rest were taken into custody.[7]

Thomas Herbert makes much of the King's pleasure at being back at Windsor. He was given 'his usual bed-chamber . . . towards the far end of the castle ward'. And he was given the liberty 'to walk where and when he pleased, within the castle, and in the long terrace without, that looks towards the fair college of Eton'. 'From the terrace', continues Herbert, 'you have a delightful view of the River of Thames, of many pleasant hills and valleys, villages and fair houses far and near; so as no place in this kingdom may compare with it, save the little castle or Lodge in Greenwich Park, which has the sight of the great and noble city of London, River of Thames, and ships of great burthen daily under sail passing to and fro'.[8]

Charles spent Christmas Day at the Castle and, although he was denied 'mince pies and plum porridge', put on a new suit of clothes which had arrived for him and made as merry as was possible in the circumstances. He was at Windsor for almost four weeks. The strictest security was maintained throughout. The Castle garrison was re-inforced by three companies of foot, and Col Harrison was ordered to keep three or four troops of horse in readiness near Windsor. Although Col Whichcot, the Governor, had general charge of the King, first Col Harrison and then Col Matthew Tomlinson were in charge of the security arrangements. The number of the King's personal attendants was reduced to six, the door of his room was constantly guarded, visitors were debarred. So that, although the King was not actually subjected to physical discomfort, his confinement was as strict as it could be made.

Meanwhile arrangements had been going ahead for the King's trial. Suggestions had been made and seriously considered that the trial should be held in Windsor Castle itself.[9] This would have solved the problem of security. There was a precedent; Mary, Queen of Scots, Charles' grandmother, had been tried and executed in the privacy of Fotheringay Castle. The Parliamentary and army leaders, however, wanted the trial to take place in the full light of day and Westminster Hall seemed the appropriate place. As Harrison proudly declared at his own trial at the Restoration, the execution of Charles I 'was not a Thing done in a Corner'.

So on 19 January the King was taken from Windsor to London. Thomas Herbert tells us how 'he took coach near the Keep . . . a guard being made all along of muskets and pikes; both officers and soldiers expressing civility as he passed by; and at the great gate a party of horse, commanded by Col Harrison, were drawn up in the market place at Pease-cod-street End'.[10] Harrison's cavalry closed round the coach and, with its six horses, it clattered down the hill beneath the Castle walls—the 'King's highway leading to the Thames', as they called it—across the old timber bridge into Eton and so over the frost-bound roads towards London. By dusk Charles was at St James' Palace.

70

His trial began in Westminster Hall on the following afternoon, 20 January. Ten days later he met his death on the scaffold in Whitehall with courage and dignity.

Cornelius Holland was one of the Commissioners for the King's trial and is recorded as being present at several of the sessions. The Clarendon papers say he had a chief hand in preparing the charges against the King. When, however, the warrant for the King's execution was drawn up on the 29th, Holland did not sign. Was it a case of cold feet at the eleventh hour? Was it illness, or some overriding personal reason? The records do not say. Almost all of Holland's closest colleagues signed, including his son-in-law Henry Smith, who was the member for Leicester. Yet within a matter of days Holland was taking a leading part in the establishment of the Commonwealth.[11]

For several days the King's body remained at St James' Palace while the debate about the place of his burial proceeded. A possibility was the vault of Henry VII's Chapel at Westminster Abbey, where James I, Henry VII himself and their Queens were interred. But a place so accessible to demonstrators and relic-hunters had obvious disadvantages. So the new rulers of the country decreed that Charles should be buried in St George's Chapel and on 7 February the cortège left London and made its slow journey to Windsor.

The story of the last rites has often been told. Four of the King's courtiers, the Duke of Richmond, the Earls of Hertford, Lindsay and Southampton were given responsibility for the obsequies. Whichcot, the Governor, held a watching brief in the background. Eventually the vault beneath the choir of St George's was located, where a century before King Henry VIII and Queen Jane Seymour, the mother of Edward VI, had been interred.

So the stage was set for the funeral on Saturday, 9 February. Richmond pleaded with Whichcot to allow Bishop Juxon, who had so often attended to the spiritual needs of the King, to read the service for the dead from the *Book of Common Prayer*. Whichcot refused because the book had been prohibited by Parliament and no amount of argument or pleading could make him change his mind.

The King's body had, on its arrival at Windsor, been taken to the hall of the Dean's house. From there it was removed to the King's bedchamber in the Castle and then again into St George's Hall. The coffin was carried to St George's by soldiers of the Garrison, the four corners of the black velvet pall being held by the four noblemen. Behind the coffin walked Bishop Juxon, carrying the *Book of Common Prayer, closed*. The rest of the King's servants followed. Col Whichcot also attended, to exercise whatever supervision was required. Snow fell on the bare heads of the mourners and on the black pall of the coffin as they neared St George's.

Inside the Chapel all was quickly over. No service was held; no prayers were said as the coffin was lowered into the vault. Those who had accompanied the King to his last resting-place turned away, while

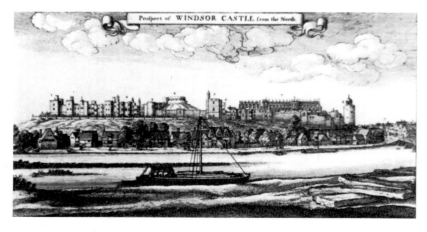

Whichcot superintended the replacing of the stones. Then the Governor and the soldiers themselves left and, beneath the majestic vaulting of the Royal Chapel, all was silent.

We are left to surmise about reactions in the town itself. We have one fact. In the Parish Register, among the records of burials, there is the simple entry for 9 February: 'King Charles in the Castle'. No legal requirement made this entry necessary. But there it stands, in between the names of Elizabeth Lyon and Mary Lee, the unostentatious record of the burial of a sometime citizen of Windsor. The townspeople had seen the King come to Windsor in December. They had seen him leave in January. Reports of the proceedings in London, sometimes confused and contradictory maybe, reached Windsor day by day. News of the execution itself would have reached Windsor speedily. The arrival of the royal cortége on 7 February would have been public knowledge. None of the townspeople was presumably allowed into the castle precincts, much less into St George's. There was no lying-in-state or filing past the coffin but, though doubtless there were men of both high and low degree who believed that the King deserved his fate, the dominant emotion must have been one of grief and shock.

ABOVE: Charles I's burial entry. BELOW: Prospect of the Castle from the north, c1670. The hamlet of Underore is shown between the Castle and the river. Windsor Bridge is on the right. An engraving by Wenceslaus Hollar. (Ashmole)

72

Commonwealth

The execution of the King was followed by the abolition of the monarchy and of the House of Lords. England became a Commonwealth, with a republican form of government. This did not make England unique. Venice, Switzerland, Holland were all republics. In a country like England, however, with its monarchical traditions extending back over many centuries, the institution of a republic was a revolutionary event.

For four years England was governed by the Rump—all that remained of the Long Parliament. The Prince of Wales, the future Charles II, was for many the rightful king. Eventually, the Commonwealth itself had to accept the establishment of 'government by a single person'. The process began when Cromwell became Lord Protector in 1653. From 1649 to 1651 he was occupied with military campaigning, first against the Irish and then against the Scots. It was not until the 'crowning mercy' of Worcester in September 1651 that the Commonwealth achieved a measure of security. Even then, another year and a half followed before Cromwell took decisive action. 'I can tell you', he said, 'what I would not have, though I cannot what I would'. By April 1653 he had come to the decision that he 'would not have' the Rump. The forcible dissolution of the Rump on Cromwell's 'day of wrath' was followed by the experiment of a nominated Parliament, Barebone's Parliament as it came to be called from the nickname of one of its members. This failed more dismally than the Rump and in December 1653, by the Instrument of Government, the Protectorate was established, with Cromwell as its head. He had less than five years to live. He wrestled manfully with his problems; in some respects he gave England (and Scotland) strong and effective government, but he was never able to govern by consent. 'I am as much for government by consent as any man', he exclaimed, 'but where shall we find that consent'? He called two Parliaments, but he had to dissolve both. For a period England was under the military government of the Major Generals. In 1657 he brought back a 'Second House' and assumed powers which, save for the title, were equal to those of monarchy. Step by step he was being driven back to the country's traditional system of government by King, Lords and Commons and, when he died on 3 September 1658, there was little justification for continuing the Commonwealth. After a further year and a half of confusion and

73

disintegration, Charles II was restored and the Puritan Revolution passed into history.

During the Commonwealth Windsor was no longer at the centre of the stage. The Castle remained a 'parliamentary' fortress, but the events by which the destinies of the country were determined took place elsewhere. An early move on the part of the House of Commons threatened to lead to the disposal of all the royal houses and parks, along with the goods and personal estate of the King, and of the Queen and the Prince. However, at the end of June 1649, the Council of State recommended that 'certain Houses and Parks be kept for the public use of the Commonwealth and not sold'. The list included 'Windsor and the Little Park near the House'.[1]

Three years later another attempt was made. In November 1652 the House of Commons resolved 'that the Castle of Windsor, with all the Houses, Parks and Lands there, belonging to the State, be sold for ready money'. A debate took place in the Commons on 29 December and as a result the decision was reversed and Windsor Castle (but not the Little Park) was excepted. The Little Park was actually sold, but subsequently re-purchased for the Protector. Windsor Castle 'and the little Park there' were reserved for Cromwell's use and pleasure.[2]

Cromwell, however, never spent much time at Windsor; he preferred Hampton Court and it is impossible to escape the conclusion that the Castle became little more than a military barracks. Provision for the continuance of the garrison was made at regular intervals throughout the Commonwealth.[3]

Even if the proposals to sell off the Castle itself (who would have bought it?) were defeated, most of the contents must have been disposed of. To the puritans, the King's pictures, sculptures, tapestries and bronzes were 'vanities'—unseemly in a godly Commonwealth. Moreover, the Commonwealth was desperately short of money. Anything that could be turned into money was sold. So the rooms of the royal palaces were stripped of their artistic glories. In December 1651 many of the hangings which still remained were removed from the Castle. They were described as 'five pieces of hanging of Triumphs, 6 pieces of David, Nathan, Abigail and Solomon, 7 of siege of Jerusalem, 5 of Goddesses'.[4] Three years later the hangings that remained were sent to adorn 'the Speaker's room adjoining the Parliament House'.[5] It is not surprising that when the diarist John Evelyn visited the Castle in 1654 he found the 'rooms Melancholy and of ancient magnificence'.[6]

The most interesting exception to the use of the Castle as a military barracks was in the provision of accommodation for the wives and children of Parliamentary soldiers who had been maimed or killed during the wars.[7] Cornelius Holland, as we have seen, had been involved in the original initiative at the time of the Civil War. This use continued right through to the Restoration of 1660. In that year, as a Petition from the Windsor Corporation to the House of Commons makes clear, there was a general eviction of these now unwanted tenants. In response to the Petition the House ordered 'that it be referred to the Justices of Peace to take care of the poor women and children, who are commanded out of the Castle of New Windsor, to dispose of the said women and children according to law'.[8]

Cornelius Holland had also played a leading part in securing provision in the Castle for 'such Soldiers as have been maimed in the Parliament's service'.[9] Cromwell seems to have followed this up and revived the institution of the Poor Knights for this purpose. When he became Lord Protector he set up a Commission of Enquiry and as a result issued an Ordinance in 1655 which read: 'We do establish thirteen Poor Knights one of them to be their governor, who have served the Commonwealth as

Elias Ashmole, Windsor historian and antiquary. After J. Riley. (NPG)

Commissioned Officers in the Army and are now out of commission and incapable of doing service either by reason of Age or by want of some limb lost in their service'. In other words the new Poor Knights were, in the phrase of the Royalist chronicler Heath, 'Cromwell's old Trojans'. Cromwell's personal interest in the scheme is apparent throughout and, when the Protector died in 1658, all the Poor Knights went up from Windsor to attend his funeral in Westminster Abbey.[10]

Cromwell increased the number of the Poor Knights from 13 to 18 and enlarged the accommodation accordingly. Charles himself had planned to increase the number and plans had been made to build a row of 'almshouses' at the foot of the Lower Ward. Sir Francis Crane had offered to advance the money, but he died before the building was carried through and lawsuits followed which effectively held up the scheme until the time of the Civil War. Now, 'Crane's Buildings' were completed and the five additional Poor Knights were given accommodation there.

The Ordinance of 1655 provided that a number of Trustees and Governors who included Bulstrode Whitelocke, the Constable, along with the Mayor and Aldermen of Windsor, were to rule and govern the scheme 'according to the statutes found among the statutes of the late dean and canons of Windsor'.[11] They were also to appoint the Knights subject to 'the recommendation, approbation or consent of the Lord Protector'. Trustees had earlier been appointed in 1650 for the sale of the lands of the dean and chapter and it was now arranged that part of the former revenues of the dean and chapter should be assigned to the Poor Knights. They were to receive '£40 apiece per annum, out of which they were to buy a gown every two years, of 4 yards of cloth, at 13s 4d per yard'.

St George's Chapel itself continued as a puritan place of worship. At the beginning of the Commonwealth the Council of State had expressed its regret to the Governor that 'there are no sermons in the Castle for the garrison and prisoners, and desire care may be taken for a supply'.[12] This state of affairs appears to have been rectified and Cromwell later instituted a regular establishment for the service of the Chapel. £100 per annum were set aside for the preacher and £40 for the weekly lecturer. He used his influence to prevent further spoliation of the chapter and their Chapel; and in 1658 the Governor was actually applying for money for the repair of the Chapel.[13]

There is no question that St George's Chapel was stripped bare by the Puritans. The charge that deliberate damage was done to the fabric itself is, however, difficult to substantiate, no matter how fashionable it may be to denounce the puritans as iconoclasts and vandals. For one thing the Chapel was clearly in need of repair before the puritan period. In 1637 Dr Wren had submitted a memorial, drawing attention to the Chapel's state of dilapidation. He particularly referred to the damage to the painted glass at the east end and said that 'whole panes were picked out'.

The finest illustrations we have of St George's at this period are the etchings of Wenceslaus Hollar, which were done for Ashmole's book on the Order of the Garter. Hollar had actually begun his sketching for the illustrations in the late 1650s, *before* the Restoration. Ashmole wrote in his diary: 'I went to Windsor, and took Mr Hollar with me to take views of the Castle'. He recorded his appreciation of the permission given him by Col Whichcot, the puritan Governor.[14] Eight of Hollar's plates show the Chapel; it is impossible to discern any damage to the stonework or even to the ornate carvings of the choir stalls in his meticulously detailed drawings.

The only possible verdict is that St George's emerged from the period of puritan ascendancy without major harm. This conclusion is strongly supported by Sir Owen Morshead, Royal Librarian for many years, in his *Windsor Castle*. With his extensive knowledge and his deep affection for St George's, it is not likely that he would defend the puritans unless he felt that his defence was justified. He writes: 'The puritans disliked stained glass; nevertheless the great west window in St George's is full today of pre-Reformation figures of saints and popes. It was their policy to destroy "superstitious pictures", but the two sequences in the Hastings and Oxenbridge chantries have survived. Up and down the country they were taking saw and hammer to angel roofs and stone carvings; yet here the carved woodwork is untouched, the tombs were spared, the 302 stone angels remain. Despite their need for metal they respected the array of Garter stallplates and the iron tabernacle-work of Edward IV's tomb'.[15]

Windsor may not have been as prominent in the events of the 1650s as it had been in those of the 1640s, but nonetheless there is no lack, in the story of Windsor in these years, of interesting representatives of the new regime. The early years of the Commonwealth witnessed, for example, the climax of Cornelius Holland's career when, as a member of the Council of State, he was in the front rank of the new rulers of the country.

The only representation of him is in a Royalist caricature of this period, showing the Devil presiding over Oliver Cromwell's Cabinet Council. Cromwell is seated at the Devil's left hand, with John Bradshaw, President of the Court which tried the King, on the right. All are listening attentively to what the Devil is saying—none more so than Cornelius Holland, who sits next to the regicide Thomas Scot. With sharp features and short pointed beard, he sits bolt upright and has his eyes fixed on the Devil. The caricaturist obviously felt he knew his man.

Only a week after the King's execution, along with Thomas Scot, Edmund Ludlow, Luke Robinson and John Lisle, he was a member of a small committee set up to draft instructions to, and nominate members of, a Council of State. Holland himself was not at first appointed to the Council, but when the nominations of Ireton and Harrison were overruled by the House, Holland and Luke Robinson were appointed in their stead. The same committee, probably under Holland's chairmanship, proceeded to consider applications for admission to the House, and on 31 May was directed to draw up a list of the absent members, and to advise the House which of them ought to be admitted and which permenently expelled.[16]

From this time on, Holland appears as one of the most energetic of the 'Rumpers'. The Rump in theory at least wanted a new and better England; in practice vested interests—especially perhaps those of the lawyers—held them back. A number of instances of Holland's zeal for reform emerge from the official reports of the proceedings of the Rump. He was one of a small group, including Alexander Rigby, Edmund Ludlow and Henry Marten, the dedicated republican member for Berkshire, who worked hard and consistently for social reform. He took a keen interest in the Rump's discussion of religious matters and was an unstinting defender of religious radicals when they were threatened with persecution. When the Rump in December 1650, in desperate financial straits, resolved to bring its separate treasuries under a single administrative body, Holland was one of those appointed finance commissioners. Earlier he had been a member of the Committee set up to investigate the debt law. He was deeply involved in the discussion of the proposals to sell Crown residences, parks and forests, including those at Windsor. He even gave his support to the melting down of cathedral bells to make ordnance for shipping, but on this he was defeated.[17]

A less attractive side of Holland's character is portrayed in the allegations that he turned his service for the Parliamentary cause to his own financial advantage. He was certainly not alone in combining puritan zeal with an eye to the main chance. Lucrative offices, including the keepership of Richmond Park, were bestowed on him. He was constantly pursuing claims arising from his previous offices in the household of the Prince of Wales. Several estates in Buckinghamshire came into his hands, including the Creslow estate, near Whitchurch, said to be worth £1,600 or £1,800 per annum. He is accused of the destruction of the chancels of a number of Bucks churches, including Winslow, Addington, East Claydon and Granborough—a formidable charge sheet.[18] One man who was no doubt glad to see the back of Cornelius was Matthew Clark, royal coachman, who in 1658 anticipated events by writing to the future King and asking for 'the keeping of your pastures of Creslow, co. Bucks, near where I was born, now held by Cornelius Holland, when it shall please God that you are restored'.[19]

Neither did Holland neglect his family interests. He had 10 children and gave one of them (possibly Elizabeth, wife of John Sheldon of West Bromwich) a marriage portion of £5,000. Another daughter married Henry Smith, who became a colleague of his father-in-law in the Rump, and gave him consistent support. 'They come in couples', wrote Clement Walker, one of the members imprisoned at the time of Pride's Purge, 'more than unclean beasts to the ark'.[20]

We do not know if Holland was present at Cromwell's dissolution of the Rump in April 1653. He does, however, disappear into the background for the whole period of the Protectorate. He could well have

John Maitland, Earl of Lauderdale, was a prominent Royalist prisoner in the Castle; minister to Charles II after the Restoration. (NPG)

been ranked as one of the fiery spirits that Cromwell preferred out of the way.

He re-surfaced briefly with the recall of the Rump in 1659, and was appointed a member of the Committee to consider 'the Settlement of the Government of this Commonwealth',[21] but along with many others he was soon submerged beneath the tides of Royalist sentiment that led to the Restoration in the following year.

Christopher Whichcot, appointed in place of John Venn in June 1645, continued as Governor of Windsor Castle throughout the whole period of the Commonwealth and Protectorate. This, in a period of frequent changes of fortune, was a remarkable achievement in itself and bears witness to the respect in which he was held. He gives the impression of carrying out his duties conscientiously, and having the trust of the Parliamentary and army leaders with whom he had to deal. He could be unyielding in his interpretation of his duties at a time like that of the King's burial. One of his most exacting responsibilities was acting as Warder for the many distinguished prisoners confined in the Castle, but even in this sphere he never seems to have attracted the opprobrium that was heaped on Venn. He survived the troubles arising from the dissatisfaction of the soldiers at their arrears of pay and that of the townspeople who had to endure nearly 20 years of the burden of quartering. He was a frequent recipient of the hospitality of the Mayor of gifts of sack and sugar loaves. And, when the short-lived Parliament during the protectorate of Cromwell's son, Richard, was chosen, Whichcot was one of the two MPs for Windsor.

Even during the Commonwealth the Governor could not relax his vigilance. There is a curious story of a Leveller plot to seize the Castle in September 1649. Several members of the garrison had been won over and were ready to admit the Levellers into the Castle 'by a certain door', which is mentioned rather mysteriously in the messages. After earlier warnings the Council of State sent a message to Whichcot on the 19th: 'We have fresh information that the Levellers intend this night to make an attempt upon Windsor Castle; we again give you this notice, as many are come out of town thither about it. We enclose an extract of a piece of intelligence brought us, by which you may discover, perhaps, who have been practising about that business, by considering who have been instruments in making or preparing that door'. On this, as at other times later, the Commonwealth Government's intelligence service seems to have been more than equal to the occasion.[22]

Whichcot had many prisoners placed in his charge. From December 1648 to January 1649 the King himself had been a prisoner at the Castle. When he was received by the Governor on his arrival, he asked about the other prisoners there and Whichcot, who seems to have discharged his duties with considerable skill, gave him the information he requested.

A final group of Royalist prisoners, all Scots, came to Windsor in 1656-7. Most of them had been captured at Worcester in September 1651, but had first been imprisoned in the Isle of Wight. They included the Earl of Lauderdale, later notorious minister of Charles II, the Earl of Crawford, Lord John Sinclair and James Wemys, Master-Gunner of England and General of the Artillery in Scotland.

Cromwell's victory at Worcester completed the triumph of the Commonwealth. Only isolated pockets of resistance in the Channel Islands and elsewhere remained to be dealt with. The number of Royalist prisoners at Windsor thenceforward was small.

Sir Richard Browne commanded Windsor Regiment during the Civil War; he was later a prisoner in the Castle. (NPG)

81

Special interest therefore attaches to the Parliamentary prisoners in the Castle. At the time of Pride's Purge, several of the Parliamentary generals were imprisoned to guard against the danger of the Presbyterians raising a rival army. They included Sir William Waller, one of Parliament's most distinguished generals in the first years of the war, and Major-General Sir Richard Browne, who had commanded the Parliamentary forces in the Midlands for some months. Ironically, Whichcot had served under Waller and must have known Browne, who amongst his other commands was in charge of the Windsor Regiment in 1644. Waller, Browne, and others were brought to the Castle on 26 January 1649. Waller's letters from Windsor bear the impress of the high-minded Puritan he always showed himself to be. In one to Sir Robert Harley in June 1649 he wrote: 'It is the chemistry of a good Christian to extract good spirits out of the evils of this world'.[23] Waller and his companions remained until 1651, when in consequence of alleged designs on Windsor they were dispersed to different castles.

A very different group comprised the Fifth Monarchy Men, who believed in the early realisation of the millenium when Christ was to establish on earth 'the fifth monarchy' in fulfilment of the prophecy of Daniel. One whom it was impossible to silence was Christopher Feake. He had called Cromwell 'the most dissembling and perjured villain in the world'. His friend and fellow prisoner at Windsor, John Rogers, had been even more precise in his condemnation and had demonstrated that 'Cromwell had broken the first eight commandments; and time alone prevented him from proceeding to the other two'. Feake wrote the story of his confinement at Windsor in a booklet called *The Oppressed Close Prisoner in Windsor Castle* (1655).[24] He describes how from 'his prison watch tower' he preached out of the window to the soldiers who were guarding him. Col Whichcot did his best to silence him. He caused drums to be beaten 'to drown the sound of the gospel'. Feake's flow of eloquence continued, however, until the Governor in exasperation 'strictly required me to have done; I told him I would not. He said he had orders to silence me from the Lord Protector. I told him I had order from my Lord to go on; and my Lord's highness is above his lord's highness'. Whichcot on another occasion had to hale him out of St George's when he anticipated the minister, and began preaching himself. 'Strange government', concludes Feake, 'that men's mouths must be stopped'.[25]

Another Fifth Monarchy man, who was brought to Windsor about the same time as Feake and Rogers, was Lord Thomas Grey of Groby, son of the Earl of Stamford. As a young man he had commanded the army of the Midland Counties Association for Parliament and had taken part in many engagements during the Civil Wars. Member of Parliament for Leicestershire in the Long Parliament, he took an active part in Pride's Purge, was one of the judges at the King's trial and signed the death warrant. He never did things by halves—his signature in bold handwriting comes immediately after that of Bradshaw, the President of the Court, and before that of Cromwell. He fought against the Scots in 1651.

Finally he joined the Fifth Monarchy Men—their creed suited his ecstatic temperament—and in February 1655 was arrested on Cromwell's orders and taken as a prisoner to Windsor. He was released in July and from this time until his death in 1657 took no active part in politics.

This by no means exhausts the list. Another prominent Parliamentarian at Windsor was Nathaniel Rich, who had given

Philip Herbert, Earl of Pembroke, was Constable of Windsor Castle 1648-50. After Van Dyke. (NPG)

distinguished service and was a republican enthusiast. Clarendon's typically caustic comment was that he was 'eminent for praying but of no fame for fighting'.[26] He became an open opponent of the Protector's government and in 1655 was arrested on a charge of stirring up disaffection. There was Cornet Day, committed to Windsor in 1656 for distributing a seditious paper in Westminster Abbey. There was Judge David Jenkins who was at Windsor from 1652 to 1657 and devoted most of his imprisonment to writing accounts, in Latin and French, of 800 leading cases in common law. There was at least one lady, Elizabeth Carey, who was intercepted carrying Royalist messages.[27]

One of the last, but certainly not the least, of the prisoners with whom Whichcot had to deal was George Villiers, second Duke of Buckingham, son of the favourite of James I and Charles I. He had tried to keep in with both sides and to effect a reconciliation between the Royalists and the Commonwealth. He returned to England in 1657, hoping to gain Cromwell's pardon. His political activities were accompanied by a romantic love affair with Mary Fairfax, daughter of the General, which led to marriage. Buckingham attracted suspicion, was arrested, sent to Windsor and later, in August 1658, to the Tower.[28]

The position of Constable of Windsor Castle was a separate office from that of Governor, involving responsibilities in the Park and Forest as well as in the Castle. It was more honorary in nature than that of Governor, not necessarily demanding residence at Windsor.

During the Commonwealth the office was held by two distinguished personalities. The first was Philip Herbert, Earl of Pembroke, who succeeded the Earl of Holland in 1648 after the latter's defection and execution and held the office until his own death in 1650. Like the Earl of Holland, he had also been a courtier, a favourite first as one of James I's handsome young men and then of Charles I, whose Lord Chamberlain he became. Pembroke – he succeeded to the earldom in 1630 – frequently entertained Charles and Henrietta Maria at Wilton House, his great mansion near Salisbury, where Van Dyke's portraits of himself and his family still adorn the walls. Like the Earl of Holland he supported the Parliamentary cause when the critical decision had to be made. Unlike the Earl of Holland, however, he maintained his support. Uncouth in manners and violent in language, he was far removed from the popular image of a puritan, but Parliament could hardly fail to welcome the adhesion of a personage of such social importance. In the month after the King's execution he became a member of the Council of State and, when the House of Lords was abolished, was one of a small number of Parliamentary peers who got themselves elected to the House of Commons—in Pembroke's case, as an MP for Berkshire.

About 1647 a disastrous fire destroyed most of Wilton House and Philip immediately commissioned Inigo Jones, the architect of Whitehall Palace, to re-build it. The work was not completed until 1653, by which time both the Earl and Inigo Jones were dead. Wilton House, however, with the gilded magnificence of its state rooms and its Van Dyke paintings, is the outcome of their partnership. It is strange, though, that the re-building should have been carried through in the troubled years following 1647, when Pembroke was Constable at Windsor Castle and the rooms there were being systematically stripped of their treasures.

Soon after his appointment at Windsor, Pembroke appointed as Deputy Governor of the Castle and Lieutenant of Windsor Forest a man who was one of the most remarkable personalities to emerge on the Parliamentary side, Bulstrode Whitelocke. His biographer, Ruth Spalding, calls him *The Improbable Puritan*. Whitelocke rode every

Bulstrode Whitelocke, Constable of Windsor Castle under the Commonwealth. (Mansell Collection)

change of circumstance with an infallible instinct for survival. He played an important part in negotiations with the King during the Civil War without compromising his position as a leading Parliamentarian. He made himself conspicuously absent at the time of the trial and execution of the King and survived to be the friend and confidant of Cromwell. He succeeded Pembroke as Constable of the Castle at some time after the latter's death and, although he lost his position at the Restoration, he blithely offered the benefit of his advice to his Royalist successor, Viscount Mordaunt. Prince Rupert also consulted Whitelocke in 1671 about the duties of the office of Constable to which he had been appointed three years before. While many of his colleagues from the revolutionary period were put to death, imprisoned or languished in exile, Whitelocke, although in straitened circumstances, survived in freedom until his death in 1675.

Whitelocke was a man of many parts. He was one of the leading lawyers of the Commonwealth and a Commissioner of the Great Seal. He was a member of both Cromwell's Parliaments and later of his 'Second House'. The most colourful episode of his colourful career was his service as Cromwell's ambassador at the Court of Queen Christina of Sweden. Christina, renowned as something of a 'blue stocking', developed a strong liking for Whitelocke. He carried out his duties as ambassador with great panache, priding himself that he could show the Swedish court that a puritan could possess all the graces of a cavalier.

Bulstrode Whitelocke had many associations with Windsor. He was a country squire, residing at Fawley near Henley where his house was ransacked early in the Civil War by Royalist troops. He came from a puritan family—his father was a judge—and sat in the Long Parliament for Marlow. Richard Winwood, the colleague of Cornelius Holland as MP for Windsor, was his life-long friend. Whitelocke often stayed with Winwood both at Ditton Park near Slough and, during the war, at Highgate whence he daily rode into Westminster.

He had a love common amongst country gentlemen—Royalist or Parliamentarian—for hunting. In September 1651 he was one of Parliament's four Commissioners sent to greet Cromwell on his triumphal return from Worcester. The Commissioners met Cromwell a few miles beyond Aylesbury and, after delivering Parliament's congratulations, they all went hawking at Windsor, with falcons provided by Winwood. His office as Constable gave him the freedom of the Park and Forest. As early as the summer of 1649, staying at the Manor Lodge in the Great Park, he enjoyed the hunting in spite of 'the best stags being all destroyed'. He resisted Cromwell's plans to carve out farms for his soldiers in the Park and Forest.

Yet another Commonwealth leader visited Windsor in 1656 and received hospitality from the Corporation. He was William Goffe, Cromwell's Major-General for Berkshire, Surrey and Hampshire during the period of military rule between the first and second Protectorate

Parliaments. Goffe had been an officer in the New Model Army, a prominent figure in the meetings of Army officers at Windsor in 1647-8 and a signatory to the King's death warrant. He commanded Cromwell's own regiment at Dunbar in 1650 and remained a staunch and trusted supporter of the Protector. In 1657 he became, like Whitelocke, a member of Cromwell's Second House. As Major-General he was, although active on behalf of the government, less arbitrary than many of his colleagues.

At the Restoration he became a marked man but, with Edward Whalley, a cousin of Cromwell and also a Major-General, he made his escape to New England where, although he found friends among the inhabitants of the puritan colony, he was constantly in danger of being arrested and sent back to England. Consequently much of the remainder of his life—he did not die until about 1679—was spent as a fugitive among the hills and forests of America.

Beneath the Castle walls the routine of life continued in the town. There must have been stress and strain, probably much grumbling at the increase of taxation and the imposition of fresh burdens and restrictions. Taxes, for example, were regularly levied for 'the maintenance of the Armies and Navies of this Commonwealth'. On the surface, however, the municipal administration appears to have pursued an uninterrupted course. The first Hall or Council Minute Book which has come down to us begins in 1653 and, although the entries are sometimes disappointingly sketchy, at least they continue from year to year and record the succession of Mayors, the appointment of Corporation officers, charities, legal proceedings, and the granting of leases.

The Hall Book gives the names of 32 members of the Council during the Commonwealth period. The trades and professions of 27 of these can be ascertained and of these no fewer than 10 were chandlers. The others included: innholder, vintner 3; butcher 1; draper, haberdasher 2; plumber 1; baker 1; tailor 2; maltster, brewer 3; physician, apothecary 3; blacksmith 1. The numbers present at meetings (where the names are given in full) compare with those after 1660 eg: 18 on 7 April 1657; 19 on 27 Nov 1658. More often the records are less specific and merely say: 'the Mayor and the greater number of the Company' (16 Nov 1657), 'the major part of the Company' (16 April 1658), 'the Mayor and Twenty others' (30 Dec 1658), 'The Mayor and the whole Company' (2 April 1660).[29]

One action of the Commonwealth government which obviously caused alarm was the calling in of the charters, a demand that was interpreted as a threat to the privileges of the Corporation. A Committee of the Rump in September 1652 had been directed to amend all borough charters after deciding 'how corporations may be settled as may be suitable to . . . the government of a Commonwealth'.[30] In 1658 the Hall Book records that 'the two charters of King James and King Charles and the copy thereof in English' should be taken away from the Treasury House and delivered to Mr Starkey, the Under-Steward. The long delay suggests considerable resistance on the part of the Corporation. It looks, however, as if the Town got its Charter back safely, for the chamberlain's accounts record that the Mayor received 1s 'for bringing the Charter from London'.

The chamberlain's accounts, after an interval of some six years, had been resumed in 1653. Many items refer to the hospitality dispensed by the Mayor and Corporation, the cost of which was entered meticulously. The usual gifts consisted of sack and sugar loaves, although Whitelocke on more than one occasion also received a barrel of ale. Sack, imported from Spain and the Canaries, was a choice white wine. Sugar also had to be imported and there were sugar bakers to make it into loaves, which were obviously highly esteemed. Proclamations were duly made according to traditional practices. In the chamberlain's accounts for 1656-7 is the item: 'Paid to the officers for a proclamation expenses and nailing the Proclamation up, 1s 1d'. When Cromwell's position was exalted in 1657 there is a whole series of entries:

'Paid for expenses at the proclaiming the Lord Protector   11s 6d
paid for deal boards and nails for the proclamations   10d
paid at the proclaiming the Lord Protector   £1 7s 4d
paid then to the Ringers   2s 0d
paid for the bonfire then   2s 6d

Soon afterwards Cromwell visited Windsor and the welcome of the Corporation cost them £1 1s 9d. Could a king have wished for more?

The Corporation was not in a healthy financial state during these years. Revenue had dropped considerably as a consequence of the political disturbances of the time. Nonetheless money had to be found for a number of necessary works. In 1649 the mediaeval town bridge, which was frequently in need of repair, was practically re-built, 'being all taken up and new planked and treble Railed throughout . . . and a new Draw bridge made at the end next unto the Town of Windsor, and some new piles where need was'. There were also extensive repairs to the Market House in 1656 and the 'Market Place' itself was enlarged two years later.

The Parish Church continued as a puritan place of worship. Soon after Charles' execution, Cornelius Holland and some of his friends in the Rump secured a measure which required the removal of the royal arms in public places. In accordance with this the King's Arms were taken down in the Church—and no doubt elsewhere. The royal insignia on the mace were probably hammered out; that at least seems the implication of the later description that the mace was 'much bruised and squatted'. In 1650 a more dramatic assertion of puritan practice occurred when the organ, presented to the Church in 1633 by Bishop Goodman, was removed. The churchwardens' accounts record:

'Recd of William Coles for four organ pipes that were left of the organ taken down in the Church, with organ pipes weighed 44 lbs sold at 7d the pound   £1 5s 10d
recd of John Cones for the wooden pipes   5s 0d

88

No new Vicar was appointed in succession to John Cleaver. There were resident 'Ministers'; from 1649 to 1653 there are references to Robert Bacon 'Minister of New Windsor'.[32] Dr George Evans who, after the Restoration, became a Canon of St George's, probably occupied a similar position in the later years of the Commonwealth. But other Ministers came to preach from as far away as Bristol and they were always provided with hospitality. Sack was the usual refreshment. One pint seems to have been the ration per minister per sermon. The cost per pint in 1650 was 8d; by 1653 it had risen to 1s, but this remained the price until the Restoration. The accounts also record from time to time the purchase of new hour glasses for the pulpit. The churchwardens' accounts, not surprisingly, do not say whether these purchases were made necessary by the vehemence of the preaching or the effect of the sack on the occupant of the pulpit!

The enforcement of the puritan code of morality was given high priority. Swearing was punished by a 6d fine and the number of entries in the accounts suggest that this was a steady source of revenue. On the other hand there seem to have been no fines for non-attendance, as earlier in the century. The pillory, depicted in Norden's view, was still in use apparently and occasionally needed repair.

In October 1653 the church plate was delivered to the Mayor and Corporation to be kept by them in the Guildhall. This was done 'for the more safe custody thereof'. It consisted of two silver flagons, two chalices, one silver cover and one bread plate. Presumably these were not needed by the puritan churchwardens and so remained with the Corporation until 1660.

The adjoining parish of Clewer, now a part of Windsor, also seems to have been staunchly puritan. The Rectors from 1603 to 1660 were a father and son, Hugo and Jacob Jones, and there is little doubt about their puritanism. Belonging to this period is the memorial on the south wall of the chancel of the ancient church to Lucie Hobson, who died in 1657. Its words have an unmistakeably puritan ring: 'She was a trew lover of a Godly and a Powerful Ministry, a Despiser of Ye World and a High Prizer of Ye Lord Christ in whose faith she lived and died in hope of a joyful resurrection with Him to whom be glory'.

Those who were faithful to the old order had to lie low and hope for better times. Bishop Brian Duppa said, 'I secure myself the same way as the tortoise doth, by not going out of my shell'.[33] Many churchmen followed Duppa in a 'tortoise' policy.

Cromwell's death in September 1658 was followed by a period of confusion, which was made worse by the refusal of Commonwealth leaders to declare themselves openly. General Monk, whose march from Scotland to London paved the way for the Restoration, did not ostensibly come to put Charles II back on the throne. He declared for a 'free Parliament'. A Parliament freely elected meant the inevitable return of the monarchy. This was what Cromwell had known and feared. A 'free Parliament' and the maintenance of the Commonwealth were incompatible.

Nevertheless the call for a 'free Parliament' had a popular ring about it and it was used not only by those who wanted to restore the monarchy but also by those who wanted to prevent the restoration or, at least, keep their options open. There is a strange episode in the Windsor story that has to be seen against this background.

The central figure in the episode is John Wildman, the Leveller, who was prepared to ally with anyone at any time in order to secure the setting up of a 'free commonwealth'. Henry Hallam, the 19th century historian, refers to him as 'one of those dark and restless spirits who delight in the deep game of conspiring against every government'. In December 1659, after a series of labyrinthine intrigues which deceived even the Royalists, he seized Windsor Castle in the name of the English republic. He tried to secure the co-operation of Whitelocke as Constable, but Whitelocke smelt a rat and refused. Governor Whichcot, however, was more gullible. Wildman gained the assistance of two veterans of the New Model Army, Col Henry Ingoldsby and Major Huntingdon, and with 300 volunteers they marched to Windsor. Whichcot agreed to surrender the Castle to them on behalf of the Commonwealth.

The recalled Rump thanked Wildman and his friends for their services. There was some suggestion that Wildman might be made Governor, but in fact Whichcot was confirmed in his governorship. This mystifying episode typifies the twilight of the Commonwealth. It has a faintly dramatic flavour, but it led nowhere.[34]

No Parliamentary elections had been held in Windsor since 1641. By the Instrument of Government which established the Protectorate in 1653, Windsor was deprived of its independent representation. This was in accordance with the desire to reform the representative system and end the representation of small or decayed boroughs. So, of the seven members allotted to Berkshire, Reading and Abingdon alone were represented separately, with one member apiece, while the remaining five represented the county—including Windsor. After Cromwell's death, however, representation was restored to the counties, cities and boroughs 'as anciently accustomed'. So Windsor regained its separate representation. In December 1658 a writ was issued for the election of two members for Windsor to the Parliament summoned during the short protectorate of Cromwell's son, Richard. Along with Col Whichcot, George Starkey, who had been Windsor's Recorder and Under-Steward for most of the Commonwealth, was returned.

Subsequent events followed a tangled sequence. This last Protectorate Parliament was dissolved in April 1659. Then the Rump was restored, with Cornelius Holland taking his seat again after an interval of six years. In February 1660 the members excluded at the time of Pride's Purge were re-admitted. One of these was Richard Winwood, so that in the closing days of the Long Parliament Windsor's MPs, Cornelius Holland

Prospect of the west end of St George's Chapel (Ashmole).

and Richard Winwood, were both there as they had been in 1641.

When the election took place in April 1660 of the 'Convention Parliament' which brought back Charles II, a double return was made for Windsor. Alexander Baker and Roger Palmer were chosen by the Corporation, but Richard Winwood by the townspeople. Baker and Palmer were declared duly returned and Winwood had to wait another 19 years before he was able to return to the House of Commons.

In March a Captain Harry Nicholl appears to have been active in regaining the Castle for the King. In a petition several years after the

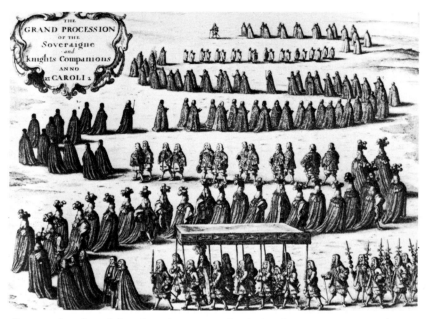

Restoration he claimed to have surprised the Castle, securing it with arms and ammunition, 'the night the General Monk broke down the City Gates'.[25]

The proclamation of King Charles II took place on 12 May and on the 25th he landed at Dover.

ABOVE: Grand Procession of the Sovereign and the Knights Companion of the Order of the Garter. (Ashmole) BELOW: The insignia of the Order of the Garter. (Ashmole)

Reftoration

Charles II returned to a joyful and welcoming country. Puritans and puritanism did not vanish into thin air, but the years of puritan ascendancy were over and the Restoration meant the return of traditional England. In Windsor the Castle once again became the Royal Castle and the town 'the King's Majesties Towne and Borough of New Windsor'.

The most vivid description of the proclamation of Charles II in Windsor comes from Windsor's senior and most respected citizen, Matthew Day. Five times Mayor and 86 years of age, he had lived through all the vicissitudes of the century. He had been a boy of 14 when the Armada was defeated. He had witnessed the coming of the first Stuart king to Windsor and had been a member of the civic party which was rebuffed by King James in the Park in 1624. He saw the rise of puritanism in Windsor and during the period of the Civil War and Commonwealth was acquainted with many of the Parliamentary leaders whose business brought them to the town. He was Mayor in 1642-3 when the Parliamentary garrison was installed in the Castle and the Parliamentary army under Essex made Windsor its headquarters. And now, in the year before his death, he witnessed the proclamation of the restored King.

'King Charles II', he wrote, 'was proclaimed King of England, Scotland, France and Ireland, upon the 12th of May 1660 at the Round Market house in New Windsor; at which time the troop of the county horse was in the Town and Mr Galland, an Innkeeper, being mayor was there attended with his Company, in their gowns, who had a Trumpeter sounding a trumpet before them; and from thence went to Windsor Bridge, and from thence went to the Castle Gate and there with the troop of horse and trumpet did likewise proclaim the King. And was desired by the officers that were in the Castle to come into the Castle and there to proclaim King Charles II in the Castle, which was also there also proclaimed with Great Joy'.[1]

The Chamberlain paid out £3 6s 3d to the Mayor for his expenses in connection with the troopers at the Proclamation.

The restoration of the royal authority was speedily recognised by the setting up of the King's Arms and within four weeks a splendid new mace had been made, carrying royal symbols and the initials CR for the new King. The old mace was pulled to pieces and openly weighed in the

Guildhall. The weight was $66\frac{3}{4}$ ounces; to this 63 ounces of silver plate were added, so that the mace was almost double in size. So urgent was the matter considered—perhaps the King was expected to visit Windsor soon—that the members of the corporation were *ordered* to disburse 10s each, 'to be repaid out of the next monies that shall come to the chamberlain's hands'.[2]

Charles II was pledged to a policy of reconciliation and in the early days of his reign he attempted to apply this policy. Only 14 persons were put to death in England, largely from the 'regicides' who had condemned Charles I. Many of those who had served the Parliamentary cause in Windsor—among them Whichcot, Whitelocke and Winwood—lived out the rest of their natural lives. Winwood even came back to be one of Windsor's MPs in the three Parliaments of 1679-81.

Cornelius Holland was one of those excepted, both as to life and estate, from the royal pardon. He had not signed the death warrant, but he had been a Commissioner for the King's trial and had been too closely involved in the King's death—'one of the late King's murderers' is a contemporary description of him—to hope for mercy.[3] However, he did not stay to crown his revolutionary career with martyrdom. On the whole he does not seem to have been the stuff of which martyrs are made. The story goes that his escape was a narrow one. He and his pursuers were both in Colchester at the same time, but with the help of a friend he was secretly conveyed out of the town and was able to reach Holland. Several of the other regicides also successfully sought refuge in the Low Countries. Among them was Daniel Blagrave of Reading. Thomas Scot, on the other hand, gave himself up to the English ambassador at Brussels and came back to face death. John Okey, John Barkstead and Miles Corbet reached Holland only to be tracked down and cold-bloodedly betrayed by an old colleague, Cromwell's scoutmaster, George Downing. All three were executed at Tyburn.

Cornelius Holland along with William Cawley, Edmund Ludlow, John Lisle and two clerks of the Court which had tried the King, John Phelps and Andrew Broughton, fled to Lausanne in Switzerland. They were allowed to remain to spend the rest of their days in exile. Lisle was stabbed and killed by an Irish Royalist one Sunday morning on his way to church. Ludlow survived until the Revolution of 1688, when he tried unsuccessfully to return to England. Of the date and circumstances of Cornelius Holland's death there is no record.

Charles and some of his advisers worked for a compromise religious settlement in 1660 which would provide liberty for tender consciences and keep at least the presbyterians inside the restored church. Several of the presbyterian leaders were offered bishoprics and, locally, Windsor's prebyterian minister, George Evans, was given a canonry at St George's. This period of appeasement was, however, short-lived. The first Parliament elected after the Restoration, the so-called Cavalier Parliament which sat from 1661 to 1679, was vehemently Royalist and

Anglican—in Macaulay's words, 'more zealous for royalty than the king, more zealous for episcopacy than the bishops'. One of its first measures was the Corporation Act of 1661 which required all members of municipal corporations to take the oaths of allegiance and supremacy ie: to swear loyalty to the King both in state and church.

This opened the door to a thorough purge of the corporations so that they would consist only of 'persons well affected to his Majesty and the established government, it being too well known that many evil spirits are still working'. The Windsor Corporation had apparently done everything within its power to express its loyalty to the restored monarchy. The attempt of the townspeople, for example, to re-assert their right to have a say in the choice of the borough Members of Parliament in the Convention Parliament of 1660 was brushed aside and in the elections for the Cavalier Parliament in the following year, the Corporation chose two Royalists, Sir Richard Braham and Sir Thomas Higgins, and the return, although challenged, was upheld.

The head of the new Restoration mace. It was made from the old mace, 'much bruised and squatted' during the Commonwealth, but was doubled in size. The initials of C.R. for Charles II are visible.

Some puritan members of the Corporation retired voluntarily; for example, Alderman Anthony Watts in September 1660.

Commissioners were nominated by the Crown to exact the required oaths from all holders of municipal office. The five commissioners who acted in Windsor were Lord Mordaunt, the new Constable of the Castle; John, Lord Lovelace of Hurley, who was one of the Members of Parliament for Berkshire; Sir Richard Braham, one of Windsor's own MPs; Sir Richard Powell of Shottesbrooke and Sir Edmund Sawyer of Heywood. No meeting of the Council is recorded after 30 September 1661 until the sessions held before the Commissioners on 14 July 1662. Four of the Council, all of them Aldermen, were ejected—John Finch, John Fisher, William Bavin and Matthew Sea. The first three were all chandlers and it was from this class of tradesmen that puritanism drew much of its strength. Steps were taken to fill the vacancies, no doubt with trustworthy persons. The next two meetings recorded in the Hall Book begin with the words 'according to the order of the Commissioners'. At the second of these meetings, on 1 September, an alderman, Henry

Fookes, who had been Mayor in 1653-4, resigned and on 13 November the under-steward, George Starkey, followed suit, neither having taken all the necessary oaths.[4]

The Corporation made application for a new Charter in 1663. This was granted in the following February and was greeted on its arrival in Windsor by the ringing of church bells. The Charter confirmed the traditional municipal constitution of the borough. Other traditional practices were restored such as the time-honoured custom of feasting. As early as September 1660 the Council had agreed that '£20 should be allowed to the Mayor for feasting to continue for seven years'.[5] No more puritan abstinence for the Corporation!

Life in the town only gradually returned to more normal ways. Quartering, which had been one of the heavy burdens imposed on the town by the puritan regimes, did not cease immediately. In November the innholders and victuallers of Windsor represented to Parliament that they were still not free from the quartering of soldiers. Three hundred, partly enlisted for the Castle, were quartered 6, 8, 10 or 12 in a house. The innkeepers had to lend them 6d a day and allow fire, candle, dressing of food, and lodging, so that 'they have few or no spare rooms, and the incumbrance will be their ruin'.[6]

For many of the ordinary people of the town the routine of life did not undergo much change. There were still poverty, disease, overcrowding, the grinding burden of unremitting labour. A petition of 1658 had called Windsor 'a great and very dear market town of 2000 people, many very poor'.[7] The Restoration clearly brought no change for the better, for a few years later, in 1666, the Corporation petitioned 'for a contribution to a design intended chiefly for his Majesty's satisfaction and that of his servants, of pitching the main streets with flint and stone; the town is much forsaken by the gentry, and the burden of the poor become so great thereby that many of the best householders leave; the town can contribute therefore little more than good wishes, hands, and spades to the work'.[8]

For the professed puritans the 'Godly Reformation' had come to a halt and those who had been the elect were now harried and persecuted. In 1662 Parliament passed the Act of Uniformity making the Prayer Book compulsory, and requiring the acceptance of episcopal ordination and of the doctrines and ceremonies of the Prayer Book from all incumbents of livings and all teachers in universities, schools and even private houses, before St Bartholomew's Day (24 August). Parliament not only threw out an attempted Toleration Act in 1663, but went on to pass two savage measures against the Puritans. The first was the Conventicle Act of 1664 which prohibited, under severe penalties, attendance at any meeting of more than four persons assembled for worship other than that of the Church of England. In the following year, when the Plague was raging in London and many Puritan ministers were returning to tend their flocks, a Five Mile Act was passed, which prohibited any of the displaced Puritan ministers from coming within five miles of a corporate town or a parish in which they had previously taught or preached, unless they swore to the Act of Uniformity or in other words abjured their puritanism.

In theory these measures ought to have crushed the puritan sects out of existence. More than 1,200 ministers left their homes and their churches by 'Black Bartholomew' rather than take the oaths of uniformity. Clewer's puritan Rector, Jacob Jones, had already gone, for his successor was appointed in 1661. He may have been actually ejected, but since he had been Rector since 1625 he was an old man by this time. In Windsor itself the Parish Church forsook what the new authorities regarded as the errors of its puritan ways. No Vicar had been appointed since the death of John Cleaver in 1648. A succession of ministers had come and gone. Now a new Vicar was appointed in Dr John Heavor. The close association between the Parish Church, St George's and Eton College continued, for like some of his predecessors he became both a

The new Charter of Charles II, 1664.

Canon of St George's and a Fellow of Eton. He was Vicar until his death in 1670 and was buried in St George's. In his will he gave £100, the interest of which was to be applied in placing out poor children in Windsor and Eton as apprentices.

Even before the new Vicar's appointment the church plate had been reclaimed, the King's arms had been restored and a *Book of Common Prayer* purchased for the Church. There was, however, a short transitional period when Dr George Evans probably continued as the resident Minister of the Parish Church. In the churchwardens' accounts for 1660-1 there is still the kind of entry familiar throughout the period of the Commonwealth: 'pd Mr Galland for xv pints of Sack given to several ministers that have preached in the parish church . . . 15s'. The fabric of the church had obviously fallen into disrepair, so much so that £24 12s 7d had to be spent on repairs in the year following the Restoration.

The records afford some insight into what happened to the Windsor puritans. Some conformed. Christopher Whichcot, puritan governor of the Castle for 15 years, was one of these. In the churchwardens' accounts for 1661 is an entry for 17s 4d from Col Whichcot for 'breaking up the ground in the church' for his son and wife. The colonel himself followed in 1664. Certainly, however, there were some who did not conform. Lord Mordaunt, the Royalist Constable of the Castle, wrote in 1661 to Sir Edward Nicholas, the Secretary of State: 'Those parts' [ie: Windsor] 'follow the example of the Presbyterians, and preach only rebellion, or if they pray for the King it is for his conversion'.[9] We have one vivid and moving glimpse into what one group of dissenters with specially strong convictions suffered. There was a group of Quakers in Windsor who met at the house of Thomas Davie (or Davey), a shoemaker. On 13 January 1661 'Came the officers and soldiers into the house of Thomas Davie, where he with his family and friends were peaceably met together to wait upon the Lord. And forced them out of the house, and had 7 of them into the Castle before the Governor, where the oath was tendered; and were Committed to prison (by the Mayor) in Windsor; and shortly after were sent to the Common Gaol at Reading. And there being many prisoners they were very Cruelly used by John Thorpe the Gaoler who shut up 22 of them in the Dungeon and several in the Wards over it, and would not suffer their friends to come to them to bring them food, and things necessary for them, for several days; and the Gaoler caused his men to take from them their Ink, and paper and knives and working tools that they might not work; and John Thorpe himself did much abuse them in words Calling them Rogues, Rebels and Traitors, and said they should all be hanged ... and 18 of the men were kept up so Close in the Dungeon within two doors that Thorpe himself Confessed he feared it would breed an Infection, being so many in that place, and though there were spare rooms enough in the wards where some were kept, yet forced so many together because they would not Satisfy his will, and give him 12d for each man a week, and find themselves straw or bedding and on the 29th ... he, with some of his Companions Came about the 9th hour of the night into the dungeon, Thorpe Calling his Companions there was not such another bed in Berkshire, and that the King would bow them and send them for a token to Venice a month hence'.[11] Quakers had been active in distributing pamphlets in Venice in 1658, but as we know from other sources it was a practice to send unwanted persons to Venice to be sold as slaves.

There were certainly Presbyterians, Independents and Baptists in Windsor, after the Restoration. A certain Samuel Smith, ejected from Bodinham in Herefordshire at the Restoration and then from St Olave's, Southwark, in 1662, afterwards became pastor of a small congregation of Dissenters in Windsor, but in what year he settled there or whether he was the instrument of collecting the society together are unknown.

We also have a record in 1667 of a conventicle of 100 or more which met constantly at the house of Samuel Price of Frogmore. Three years

Prospect of the inside of St George's Chapel at the Restoration. (Ashmole)

later a licence for Presbyterian services was granted for 'the house of Jane Price in New Windsor, Berks'. Probably Samuel Price was dead and this lady was his widow. The application was for 'Mrs Jane Price's new house called Frogmore'. We know also from a return sent into Archbishop Sheldon in 1676 that the number of dissenters in Windsor was 115 out of 1,025 adults—the highest in Berkshire.[11] At least it is certain that puritan dissenters survived the intolerance and the persecution of the Restoration years, but they never again became dominant in the town. Windsor became and remained predominantly Royalist and Anglican.

Charles II developed a great affection for Windsor and from 1670 he normally spent a portion of every summer there. In the early years, however, there was little to attract him to the Castle, left desolate and bare by the depredations of the Commonwealth period. Work began on the Castle immediately after the Restoration. Much of the furniture and many of the hangings were recovered. £2,000 was spent in preparing lodgings for King Charles and Queen Catherine, the Portuguese princess whom he married in 1662. Even in 1670, however, John Evelyn recorded in his diary that the Castle was 'exceedingly ragged and ruinous'.[12] At the same time, however, Evelyn referred to the plans for the repair of the Castle. These plans in fact amounted to much more than repair, rather a transformation of a feudal fortress into a palace. Many parts of the Castle, especially in the Upper Ward, were virtually re-built; the present State Apartments were fashioned and the Terrace extended from the northern front to the eastern and southern sides.

Nothing on so extensive a scale was attempted again until Wyatville's reconstruction of the Castle in the time of George IV. The architect was Hugh May—Christopher Wren only came in at a later stage—and the two most notable craftsmen were Grinling Gibbons, whose intricate wood carvings adorn many of the state rooms, and Antonio Verrio, the Italian artist who covered the ceilings with his colourful mythological extravaganzas. Over the years the rooms were filled with pictures and tapestries so that, although Charles could not go all the way in emulating Versailles, at least he made Windsor Castle a finer royal residence than it had ever been before.

The King, in the early years after his Restoration, used Windsor for the same two main purposes that his father had done—hunting and the Garter ceremonies. The latter had always, since the institution of the Order by Edward III in 1348, been associated with Windsor, and particularly with St George's Chapel. The Civil Wars and Commonwealth had meant a long interval. Charles had held chapters of the Garter from time to time during his years of exile and on 26 May 1660, the day after he landed at Dover, Monk and Montagu (who commanded the fleet which brought the King to England) were declared Companions of the Order. The first feast of the Garter after the Restoration was held on 15, 16 and 17 April 1661. The King arrived at Windsor from Whitehall on the 15th. Ashmole refers to the traditional cavalcade to Windsor: 'this Proceeding on Horseback was generally set forth with exceeding pomp'. Twelve Companions were installed with all the historic ceremonies; They included Monk and Montagu, now respectively the Duke of Albemarle and the Earl of Sandwich. The Feast itself had in it, wrote Ashmole, 'all manner of magnificence and plenty, as well as of provision of all other things that could add glory thereunto'.

Much had been done to restore the dignity of the Chapel. We have seen that very little damage had been done to the structure itself during the years of puritan ascendancy, but the Chapel had been stripped of many of the accessories of church worship. From early in the reign much was done to restore the fittings to their former splendour. The Duke of York, the King's brother, gave a piece of Plate of £100 value and the other Knights-Companion followed suit, so that the Chapel acquired flagons, chalices, candlesticks, tapestries.

All of this must have been distasteful to puritans of every variety. There is a story that a certain Canon of St George's refused to bow to the altar, at which the King remarked: 'If he will not bow to God, let him not bow to me', which, the narrator noted, 'made him the more supple next day'.[13] The Canon was Dr George Evans, the presbyterian minister of the Parish Church during the Commonwealth. When the Earl of Lauderdale, himself a presbyterian, was a prisoner in the Castle, Evans visited him and a friendship sprang up between the two men which led Lauderdale to procure for Evans at the Restoration a canonry at St George's. Later Evans was Rector of St Benet's Fink, London for many years. He also became a distinguished antiquary, whose materials on the history of the Chapel are printed in Ashmole's *Antiquities of Berkshire*.

The Dean of Windsor from 1660 to 1677 was Dr Bruno Ryves. A staunch Royalist, he had been deprived of his benefices in 1642. He was the author of the violently anti-puritan *Mercurius Rusticus* and now came to preside over the restoration of St George's and the Garter ceremonies so long associated with the Chapel. He was certainly not a man who could be expected to show sympathy or tolerance towards puritans.

Cromwell's Poor Knights gave some trouble to the Royalist authorities at the Restoration. More than a year later Mordaunt was complaining that they were 'insolent, refuse commands, will not remove, and have been tampering with the soldiers.'[14] In 1662 the Dean consulted the Attorney-General about the expulsion of Captain Cave, one of the Knights, 'on account of his contempt in refusing submission'.[15]

For the Park the return of the King meant both restoration and development. Alexander Thayne, Gentleman Usher of the Black Rod, was restored to possession of the Little Park, from which he had been evicted in 1648. Charles lost no time in plans to re-stock the Park and Forest with deer. One Trumball of Easthampstead had entered into a contract, but it seems was unable to fulfil it. In November 1661, there was an order releasing him from it, and a warrant on account to Sir William St Ravy for the expenses of transporting red and fallow deer from Germany and elsewhere to replenish Windsor and Sherwood Forests.[16] A beginning was made with the plans for laying out paths, and planting the avenues which culminated in the magnificent Long Walk, begun in the 1680s. The story of the creation of the great lakes of the Park belongs, however, to the 18th century.

When Samuel Pepys visited the Park in 1665 he found it 'a very melancholy place, with little variety save only trees'. However, for Windsor itself, which he visited in the following year, he had much praise. Of St George's he said, 'It is a noble place indeed, and a good Quire of

Voices. Great bowing by all the people, the Poor Knights in particular, to the Altar'. Of the Castle he remarked, 'It is the most romantique castle in the world'.[17] What Puritan could have made that comment!

Charles II in Garter Robes. (Ashmole)

References

Abbreviations

Ash MSS *Ashmole Manuscripts,* Oxford. References are given to the reproductions of Ashmole's transcriptions in Tighe and Davis, Annals of Windsor (see below).
BRO   Berkshire Record Office.
CJ   Journals of the House of Commons.
Clar   *The History of the Rebellion,* by Edward, Earl of Clarendon, ed W.D. Mackray, 1888.
CSPD   Calendar of State Papers, Domestic Series.
HB   *The First Hall Book of the Borough of New Windsor, 1653–1725.* Published as Vol I of the Windsor Borough Historical Records Publications, ed S.M. Bond, 1968 (Windsor Records ACaI).
LJ   Journals of the House of Lords.
Luke   *The Letter Books of Sir Samuel Luke* 1644–5. Historical Manuscripts Commission 1963.
Ru   Rushworth, J. *Historical Collections 1618–1649.*
TD   Tighe R.R. and Davis J.E. *Annals of Windsor 1858.*
TT   *Thomason Tracts,* British Library.
Turner   Turner, G.L. ed *Original Records of Nonconformity under Persecution and Indulgence,* 1911.
Wh   Whitelocke, B. *Memorials of the English Affairs,* 1853 ed.

Before the Storm

1 *Ash MSS 1126. TD II.108*
2 *Windsor Borough Deeds,* Lease No 189
3 Ash MSS *op. cit.* TD II. 59–60
4 *ibid* TD II. 111–4
5 *ibid* TD I. 657
6 *ibid* TD II. 82–3
7 *ibid* TD I. 401
8 *ibid* TD I. 619–20
9 *ibid* TD I. 636
10 CSPD 1625–6. 67
11 *ibid* 1625–6. 126, 132
12 *ibid* 1636–7. 130
13 *ibid* 1625–6. 171
14 Ash MSS *op. cit.* TD II. 146
15 Ashmole, *Order of the Garter,* 136
16 qu. TD II. 77
17 Ash MSS *op. cit. TD II. 101*
18 *ibid* TD II. 100–2

The Gathering Storm

1 *CSPD 1638–9. 1, 9*
2 qu. *J.S. Morrill, The Revolt of the Provinces,* p 148
3 CSPD 1640–1. 248
4 CJ ii. 47–70 *passim* Ash MSS *op. cit.* TD II. 148–50
5 CJ ii. 158–9
6 Ash MSS *op. cit.* TD II. 149
7 qu. D. Hirst, *The Representative of the People?* App.
8 qu. J.S. Morrill *op. cit,* p 148
9 Clar xi. 104
10 CJ ii. 282
11 LJ iv. 595
12 CSPD 1641–3. 346

13 LJ iv. 653
14 Clar iv. 196, 200, 210 CSPD
    1641–3, 252–281 *passim*
15 Clar iv. 229. LJ iv. 523–4
16 Clar iv. 217
17 Clar iv. 275
18 Clar iv. 301. CSPD 1641–3. 273
19 CSPD 1641–3. 281

The Storm Breaks

  1 CJ ii. 671
  2 CJ ii. 768
  3 TT. E123 (20)
  4 CJ ii. 811
  5 TT. E123 (20) *op. cit*
  6 Clar vi. 216
  7 TT. E126 (42); E127 (10)
  8 Ru III. 58
  9 Clar vi. 133, 134
10 Clar vi. 154
11 Clar vi. 155
12 Clar vi. 207
13 TT. E85 (6)
14 qu. O. Morshead, *Royalist
    Prisoners*, p 11
15 qu. Morshead *op. cit.* pp 9–10
16 *ibid* p 4
17 CJ 1643, ii. 922, 928, 952
18 *The Knyvett Letters*, ed B.
    Schofield, pp 114–6

Fortunes of War

  1 qu. TD II. 89
  2 LJ vi. 30
  3 CJ iii. 341, 348
  4 CJ iii. 40; LJ vi. 30
  5 LJ vi. 30, 44, 57, 59
  6 See TD II. 159
  7 CSPD 1641–3. 474
  8 LJ vi. 21
  9 LJ v. 719; vi. 39, 77, 111; vii. 7,
    281–3, 509, 510
10 CJ iii. 495
11 CJ iii. 458. CSPD 1644. 108,
    110, 437
12 CJ iii. 681–2, 697–9 CSPD
    1644–5, 124, 130, 138
13 CJ ii. 896
14 qu. TD II. 187 fn
15 CJ iii. 199
16 CSPD 1644–5. 69, 78, 109,
    118–9
17 *ibid* 121, 129, 266, 347, 364, 369,
    394, 396
18 CSPD 1645–7. 217

Rendezvous at Windsor

  1 J.W. Fortescue, *A History of the
    British Army*, 1899 p 213

  2 qu. J. Adair, *John Hampden*,
    p 214
  3 *Reliquiae Baxteriana*. I. 48
  4 J. Sprigge, *Anglia Rediviva*, p 10
  5 Ru IV. 16–7
  6 Wh I. 136
  7 Luke. Letter 517
  8 Wh I. 190
  9 Luke. Letter 700
10 TT. E392 (6)
11 TT. E318 (6)
12 C.H. Firth, *Cromwell's Army*.
    App I, p 409
13 LJ vii. 256
14 Firth *op cit*, pp 247–8
15 CJ iv. 126
16 CSPD 1644–5. 446, 513–5, 547
17 Luke. Letter 576 Sprigge *op cit*,
    p 15
18 Ru VII. 140

Untrodden Paths

  1 CJ iv. 198
  2 LJ viii. 247, 260 CJ iv. 399, 468,
    502, 631
  3 Ru VI. 647
  4 Ru VII. 921
  5 CJ v. 376
  6 Tanner MSS, qu. TD II. 223
  7 CJ v. 575–6
  8 CSPD 1648–9. 204
  9 LJ x. 211
10 CSPD 1625–49. 643, 668–9
11 CJ v. 421
12 CJ iii. 693
13 Luke. Letters 404, 470, 1181
14 Clar x. 93
15 Ludlow, *Memoirs* I. 174
16 Ru VII. 913
17 Ru VII. 953
18 Ru VII. 951
19 TT. E979 (3)

This Great Business

  1 CSPD 1648–9. 142, 152, 168
  2 CSPD 1648–9. 246
  3 see M.A. Gibb, *John Lilburne*,
    p 238
  4 Clarke Papers, ed C.H. Firth, II.
    53
  5 Ludlow, *Memoirs*, I. 270
  6 see G.S. Stevenson, *Charles I in
    Captivity*, pp 167–171
  7 TT. E536 (1)
  8 Stevenson *Op cit.*, p 176
  9 TT. E477 (28)
10 Stevenson *op cit.*, p 181
11 CSPD 1648–9. 351

Commonwealth
1 CJ vi. 150, 189, 246, 247
2 CJ vii. 237
3 eg: CSPD 1655. 239; 1656–7.
   129
4 CSPD 1651–2. 546
5 CSPD 1654. 342
6 Evelyn, *Diary*, 8 June 1654
7 CJ vii. 857
8 CJ viii. 112
9 CJ v. 421
10 CSPD 1650. 12; 1651–2. 496;
   1655. 304; 1656–7. 216
   Heath's *Chronicle*, 1676, p 372
11 TT. E1064 (50)
12 CSPD 1649–50. 32
13 CSPD 1657–8. 311–2
14 Ashmole, *Diary*, 1927ed, p 63
   Order of Garter p 628
15 see O. Morshead, *Windsor
   Castle*, pp 102–3
16 Ludlow, *Memoirs*, I.288 CSPD
   1649–53 *passim*
17 CJ vi. 255, 280, 352; vii. 152
18 CJ iv. 270; vi. 496–7 CSPD
   1654. 127
19 CSPD 1657–8. 273
20 Clement Walker, *History of
   Independency*, i. 173
21 CJ vii. 775
22 CSPD 1649–50. 312, 314
23 Portland MSS, qu. J. Adair,
   Roundhead General, p 200
24 TT. E820 (10)
25 CSPD 1653–4. 371; 1654.
   188–9, 253
26 Clar xi. 104

27 CJ v. 648. CSPD 1656–7. 42, 71,
   112, 116, 130. 1660–1. 19
28 CSPD 1658–9. 125
29 HB 1653–60 *passim*
30 CJ vii. 178
31 Ash MSS. TD II. 264–5
32 eg: BRO. Order dated 27 Jan
   1653
33 qu. W.M. Lamont, *Godly Rule*,
   pp 154–5
34 CSPD 1659–60. 58, 60, 131,
   196, 299, 321
35 CSPD 1667. 531
Restoration
1 Ash MSS. TD II. 289
2 HB 14, 18 May; 11 June 1660
3 CSPD 1660–1. 340
4 HB 3 Sept 1660; 30 Sept 1661;
   14 July 1662
5 HB 3 Sept 1660
6 CJ viii. 184
7 CSPD 1658–9. 221–2
8 CSPD 1666. 410
9 CSPD 1661–2. 89
10 BRO D/F 2A 1/1, p 8. *Berkshire
   and Oxfordshire Quarterly
   Meeting Minute Book
   1655–1680*
11 Turner I. 112, 134
12 Evelyn, *Diary*, 28 Aug 1670
13 *The Papers of Thomas
   Woodcock* (Camden Soc 1907)
   pp 62–3
14 CSPD 1661–2. 89
15 *ibid* 518
16 *ibid* 158, 173
17 Pepys, *Diary*, 25 Feb 1666

General Note

No attempt has been made to give a comprehensive general bibliography. Books on the Civil War and Commonwealth are innumerable; many public libraries have a good selection. The *Dictionary of National Biography* is a rich source of information about many of those who figure in the book. The most detailed 'local' account is still that contained in Tighe and Davis, *Annals of Windsor*. Among the few articles relevant to the puritan period in Windsor are:

Bond, M.F. 'Windsor's Experiment in Poor Relief 1621–1829' *Berks Arch Journal, Vol 48*.

Morshead, O. 'Royalist Prisoners in Windsor Castle' *Berks Arch Journal, Vol 56*

Millar, O. 'The Inventories and Valuations of the King's Goods 1649–51' *Walpole Soc, Vol 43, 1972*

The most important of the 'original' local records extant are the First Hall Book, which begins in 1653 *(Windsor Records ACaI)*; the Chamberlains' Accounts *(Windsor Records FAc2)*; the Churchwardens' Accounts *(Berkshire Record Office D/P 149/5/1)*; and the Parish Records of the Church of St John the Baptist (also BRO, but there are copies in Windsor). All of these have gaps and deficiencies, but together constitute a wide range of source material. The invaluable Ashmole MSS, including transcriptions of Matthew Day's Book, were, as noted above, mostly reproduced by Tighe and Davis.

Index

106

108

Subscribers

Presentation Copies

1 The Royal Borough
2 Windsor Library
3 Maidenhead Library
4 Eton Library

5 Raymond South
6 Clive & Carolyn Birch
7 The Royal Library, Windsor Castle
8 M.W. Barnard
9 M.E. Barnard
10 Sandra Lewis
11 A.D.E. Catchpole
12 A. Massey
13 Mrs Helen McTiffin
14 Leslie Grout
15 Denis Shaw
16 H.C. Macey
17 Mrs C. Buck
18 Terence Emery
19 David Allen
20 S.A. Thompson
21 T.J. Greenaway
22 Peter F. Gray
23 Mrs Lydia Rath
24 K.G. Wheatley
25 Keith Cavendish-Coulson
26 Mr & Mrs E.K. Rodbard-Brown
27 E.J. Singer
28 T.A. Gosling
29 C.J. Berks
30 John Crump
31 Mrs D.M. Shakespeare
32 Mrs H. Hedges
33 P. Dennis
34 Mr & Mrs E.V. Dixon
35 David R. Dyde
36 Peter Chard
37 David Read
38 Malcolm Read
39 Victoria & Albert Museum
40 Leicester Library
41 B.S. Kiek
42 P.S. Borlase
43 J.H.A. Gibson TD
44 Mrs M.L. Dennis
45 S.G. Humphries

46 Mrs Anne Taylor
47 Miss E.W. Lerrigo
48 Mrs Susan Lupetti
49 A.H. Paul
50 G. Crowhurst
51 Kathleen Lewis
52 E.W. Fry
53 Edward Sammes
54 M.J. Beardsmore
55 L.J. Braitch
56 Janet Chowh
57 Mrs Y. Martin Holder
58 Marten Collins
59 Don & Mollie Dunning
60 Joyce & Frank Marmoy
61 Mrs M.I. Duffy
62 K.J. Fry
63 Mrs Maureen G. Buckley
64 F.J. Alderman
65 Jon Nickerson
66 Alwena & Ralph Maddern
67 Manderville School
68 Nicola Brooker
69 Mrs Muriel Stillwell
70 Mrs R.J. Learwood-Griffiths
71 Fred Price
72 C.E. Hamshere
73 W.N. Neate
74 Dr F. Henthorn
75 William A. Phillips
76 Cllr Denis J. Downham
77 J.H.M. Weston
78 Slough Teachers' Centre
79 Mrs J. Waltham
80
81 A.F. Upton
82 R. South
83
84 Brigadier P. Young
85 Brian W. Atkinson
86 L.S. Beard
87

88 Miss K.M. Shawcross
89 John E. Handcock
90 David J. Calthup
91 Ronald Edwards
92 Joe & Ruth Newman
93 John R. Newman
94 David Ronald Davies
95 Pamela Delamere
96 B.J. Morfett
97 A.E. & D.E. De'ath
98 George E. West
99 G.B. Warner
100 A.T. Pinder
101 Mrs Olive Gosling
102 Rosemary Dale
103 J.T. Clarke
104 Windsor Boys' School
105 John B. Dyson
106 W.G. Street
107 Barbara Stoney
108 Stanley F. Jones
109 P.A. Preston
110 L.W. Best
111 Dora Baker
112 Janet Mary Peterken
113 W.M. Pratt
114 John E. Finch
115 David Higgs
116 Mrs M. Colman
117 Mrs Hawkins
118 Berkshire County Library
119 Mrs A.R. Ross
120 Mrs G. Spindlow
121 D.A. Lane
122 Mrs Vanda Smith
123 Barbara Ansell
124 Stanley Brown
125 S.M. Muir-Goulding
126 Simon Bond
127 Gerry Hodes
128 Trevor Clark
130

131 Guy Bousfield	218 Miss B.M. Smith	271 Dora M. Loftus
132 Miss K. Naylor	219 R.R. Bolland	272 Colonel R.O. Mells
133 Mrs R.W. Heybourn	220 Richard Cox	273 W.J. Allen
134 Rosemary Thompson	221 Colin Oakley	274 Mr & Mrs Western
135 K.N. Bigsby	222 Derrick King	275 Mr & Mrs Entwhistle
136 Sheila Noakes	223 John Counsell OBE	276 Bulmershe College of
137 Anne Bowden	224 G.G. Windsor	Higher Education
138 N. Iley	225 Langley College of	277 J.S. Hunneman
139 J. Allbless	Further Education	278 David Thomson
140 L. Snell	226 Ethel & Bill Richards	Walker
141 Mrs M. Fountain	227 Pauline L.M. Chart	279 Marko Romanic
142 Mrs J.M. Pye	228 B.M. Douglass-	280 George R. Lawn
143 Mrs J.M. Pye	Hamilton	281 William Smith
144 David James	229 Maurice Wallace	282 Peter C. Kelsey
145 J.D. Evans	230 B.D. Webster	283 A.H.W. Sexton
146 E.G. Perry	231 Mr & Mrs George E.	284 Alan R. Titchener
147	Heape	285 Miss P. James
148 Berkshire County	232 R. Munns	286 J.A. Sharpe
176 Library	233 Susan R. Mercer	287 Raymond T. Harberd
177 Windsor College	234 David J. Perkins	288 Patrick Purchase
Library	235 Mrs Judith Hunter	289 Angela Perkins
178 Mrs C. Male	236 A.J. Littlewood	290 Pamela M. Bacon
179 Mr & Mrs M.	237 Ian A. Legge	291 Mrs S. Horder
Dickson	238 Derek R. Waters	292 Nick Falder
180 Mrs Drew	239 P.R.S. Renacre	293
181 Mrs D. Moseley	240 Mrs D. Hills	294 Miss Hazel M.
182 Mrs S.C. Handbury	241 George R. Read	Cumming
183 Mrs D. Morris	BMus	295 T.W. Taylor MVO
184 Miss S. Ralley	242 P. George	OBE
185 Mrs E. Hughes	243 R.W. Lewandonski	296 Mrs P.A. McCarthy
186	244 David Charlton	297 Dr D.K.M. Thomas
187 R. Renn	Jessey	298 Elizabeth Brown
188 L. Barker	245 Mrs S.L. Ashley	299 Tom Middleton
189 Mrs M. Fountain	246 The Bishop of	300 Mrs J.M. Beckett
190 G. Ackland	Worcester	301 Mrs S.R. Ballance
191 Dr G. Pierce	247 Irene M. Aylett	302 Sheila Wallace
192 J. Ackroyd	248 Virginia Berridge	303 Roger Cullingham
193 Mrs A. Probart	249 D.M. England	304 Mark Cullingham
194 Mrs B. E. Crook	250 Albert M. Charlish	305 Tony Bradbury
195 Martin Stone	251 D. Barnard	306 Harry J. Fenech
196 Miss Jayne Hesmer	252 G.C. Bryant	307 R.J. Wyatt
197 W.H. Dickinson	253 Robert William	308 Ernest A. Day
198 A. Garside	Portus	309 David Cawsey
199 A.L. Forster	254 W.H. Paine	310 D.R. Garrett
200 Colin M.H. Bance	255 T.W. Smith	311
201 Stewart Curtis	256 Miss E.H. Cuthbert	312 Dr & Mrs G.J.
202 Mrs G. Pettigrew	257 Stephen E. Morgan	Harrap
203 Lorna Sharpe	258 A. Pink	313 Doris Charlish
204 Miss Doris Williams	259 Alan W. Fone	314
205 Elaine Carwarding	260 Waingels Copse	315 C.G. Float JP
206 Mrs A.M. Pring	School	316 R.N. McRae
207 Rt Rev M.A. Mann	261 Kendrick Girls'	317
208 Sally Krieger	School	318 Ann Brett
209 Vera Moore	262 William M.	319 Roger Mayne
210 Cllr S.W. Andrews	Holdsworth	320 Carmel Finney-
211 Mrs C.M. Davies	263 Raymond H. Willis	321 Reg S. Stevenson
212 Mrs Glenice White	264 Peter Ellis Jones	322 Pamela May
213 Peter Darville	265 Dedworth Middle	Hockedy
214 John Rowse	School	323 Maidie L. Martin
215 R.G. & A.C.	266 Carolyn Whibley	324 Robert Jones
Beauchamp	267 Constance Denby	325 Mrs J. Leonard
216 University College	268 Grace Oddy	326 Gladys Reeves
Oxford	269 Roland Paul Snelling	327 K. Buckingham
217 Karen Farrington	270 Daniel Rosenthal	328 Peter Hjul

329 Dr C.J. Buckingham	369 Janet Emerson	406 Lady Liddell
330 Mary Stella Graham	370 Jill Moulton	407 G.S. Parker
331 N.M. Waring	371 Harold Basford	408 R.L. Bull
332 Maurice Bond	372 Library of the	409 Tim Ackland
333 A.C. Fraser	Religious Society	410 F.W. Jones
334 Elizabeth Handy	of Friends	411 Lillie F. South
335 Mrs E.G. Aldred	373 Mrs S. Pym	412 Daphne V. Fido
336 Brigitte Mitchell	374 Dr F.J. Long	413 G.M. Hall
337 Lt Col P.A. Belton	375 Mrs A.W.G.	414 Dr E.C. Willatts OBE
338	McQueen	415 A.G. Brown
339 Arthur Wells	376 Ann Timperley	416 Mrs K. King
340 Sir John Grandy	377 David Hedges	417 David Jefferson
341 Brian Galloway	378 A.W. Sampson	418 C.M. Adcock
342 Mrs M. Miles	379	419 D.A. Blundell
343 Jean M. Palmer	380 Gordon Cullingham	420 John Kemp
344 Brenda Chown-Smith	381 Rev I. Halden	421 James Kinross
345 H.B. Dunsmore	382 Miss V.J. Langton	422 Richard Shaw
346 Dedworth Middle	383	423 David J. Poynter
School	384 Z.M. Vaughan-Payne	424 Mr & Mrs Paul J.
347 Mrs Patricia Bevan	385 H. Fairhurst	Ayres
348 Joan George	386 L.M. Whittome	425 Alan Gillies
349 J.F. Hoppe	387 Marjorie E. South	426
350 A. Melluish	388 Clifford & Dorothy	428 John R. Norbury
351 C.R. Bishop	Howard	429
352 P.J.Smith	389 Rev J.E. Hirst	430 J.A. Meredith
353	390 Desmond & Joy	431 Christopher James
354 Anne Teresa Hegarty	Saunders	Gilson
355	391 Rev J. Murray	432 Brenda Wiggins
356 Windsor Boys' School	392 Edward H. Milligan	433 Marion Griffin
357 Dorothy A. Johnston	393 John Sinclair	434 Dr B.L. Thompson
358 V.S. Stoner	394 Rev D.N. Griffiths	435 Eton College Library
359	395 Rev D. Shaw	436 E. Whiteley
360 Dr H.W. Parris	396 I. Halden	437 J.C. & R. Newman
361 Brenda Williamson	397 Mrs L.M. Whittome	438 Papplewick School
362 G.C. McNeile	398 Mrs Ida Baker	439 Grace Stephen
363	399 Brian W. Atkinson	440 Liz A. Fothergill
364 B.W. Deane	400 Mrs Jean Kirkwood	441 Miss K.M. Shawcross
365 Clive Moulton	401	442 B. Williams
366 Florence Meech	402 Reginald Try	443 Major R.D. Battcock
367 Charles Stainer	403 Mrs Richard Tozer	MBE
368 Margaret & Brian	404 Eric Vesey	*Remaining names*
Whitelaw	405 Joan Smith	*unlisted.*

ENDPAPERS – FRONT: John Norden's View *of the Little Park and Town, 1607. (TD) BACK: The Castle after the Restoration, seen from the south-east. St George's Chapel and the Keep are prominent. Engraving by Wenceslaus Hollar. (Ashmole)*

111

*Windsor's Arms, as entered by William Harvey, Clarenceux
King of Arms, in 1566.*

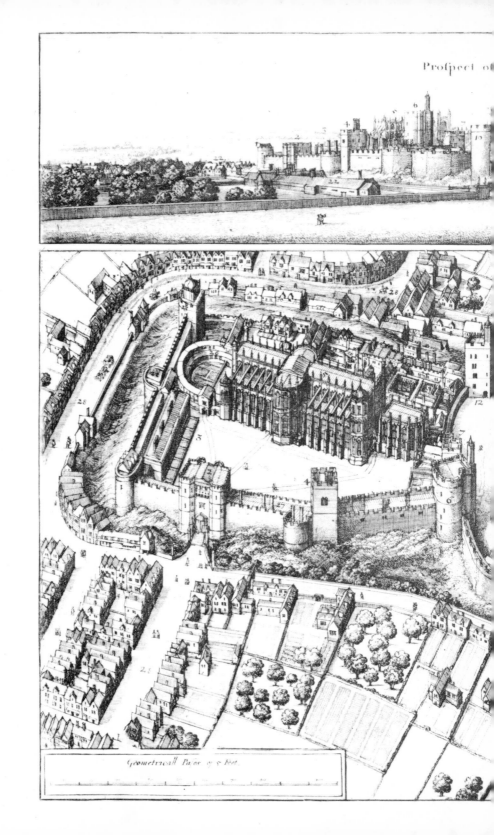

Prospect of

Geometricall Pases of 5 feet.